FUTURE PROSPECT

BY:

GLENN CALVIN DAMOND

"THE POWER OF YOUR FUTURE IS IN YOUR HANDS"

WHENEVER ORGANISMS STEP OUTSIDE OF THEIR PROPER ENVIRONMENT, THEY BEGIN TO DIE OFF.

Future Prospect, Copyright © 2014 by Glenn Calvin Damond, Relationship Guru/Inspirational speaker. All rights reserved. No part of this book may be reproduced in any form without the written permission of the publisher. For information and contact, address 3526 Huntlee Drive New Orleans Louisianan 70131.

Published in the United States by Future Prospect Book Publishing, LLC. A unit of G.C.D productions.LLC, New Orleans Louisiana.

http://www.gcdproductions.com.

Library of congress control
Number: 2014903497

Book designed by Brandon Jones for BJ Graphic

Distributed by Future Prospect book Publishing, LLC. A unit of G.C.D.

Edited By Glenn C. Damond

Future Prospect, The power of your future is in your hands---Whenever organisms step outside of their proper environment, they begin to die off. / Glenn C. Damond, Relationship Guru/Inspirational Speaker

Includes bibliographical references

ISBN: 978-0-615-97832-1   (Paperback)

PRINTED IN THE UNITED STATES OF AMERICA

First paperback Edition

CONTENT

PART ONE: Which position are you in?

1. The woman and the Lady (Which one are you?)

2. The woman and the Lady (Part 2) (Which one are you?)

3. The man verses the Gentleman

4. The man verses the Gentleman (Part 2)

PART TWO: Organisms dying off

1. Organisms dying off in their sex lives

2. Organisms dying off in their intimate relationships

3. Organisms dying off in their intimate relationships (Part 2)

4. Organisms dying off when they indulge in desired habits

PART THREE: What is the best relationship to be in?

1. Half Relationships (in the work environment)

2. Half Relationships (in your intimate relationship)

3. Half Relationships (in your intimate relationship (part 2)

4. The best relationship to be in (keys that unlock the road to a lasting intimate relationship)

5. The best relationship to be in (keys that unlock the road to a lasting intimate relationship)

(Part 2)

6. The best relationship to be in (keys that unlock the road to a lasting relationship)

(Part 3)

PART FOUR: Whenever the game is played, you will either win or lose.

1. So you want to play games?

2. When to play the game-if ever

3. The natural and the unnatural

4. The problem verses the solution

CONCLUSION... 185

BIBLIOGRAPHY..187

ABOUT THE AUTHOR..197

ACKNOWLEDGMENTS:

I acknowledge all who believe in me and the vision that God has given me. Thanks from the bottom of my heart for all your prayers and support. I originally named many names, but I knew I left some people out. So I took all names out because my team knows what it is.

INTRODUCTION:

I grew up on the dangerous streets of New Orleans Louisiana. I was in the mall one day and a recruiter of the army was in there recruiting. She asked me was I interested in joining the Army. I laughed and said I was in the army already and I had made it out with all my body parts. She then asked me where I was deployed. I said I grew up in New Orleans. She laughed and got the message and said that I was right.

My street name was La Glenn as I rose to the status of a boss player and original gangsta, in the sixth and seventh ward. I am originally from the seventh ward-that great St Bernard project.

I had no true guidance; notwithstanding, my life consisted of leadership attributes. It could have been a female or male. I could always find someone to follow me in whatever I choose to participate in. It could have been committing a crime or using drugs, I would have someone to follow me. I was leading them into destruction then.

Now that God has changed my life and embedded within me his vision. The leadership ability in me now caters to propelling people forward in the right direction.

In this book, you will learn much. You will receive a detailed understanding on how organisms (People) dying off in life in different areas of their lives. Both the bible and scientist agree and that certain organisms possess the longevity of life. This lasting life is realized when the organisms correspond with the environment suited for their existence. What do you mean Mr. Damond? I will explain to you in just a second.

Life has proven that whenever organisms are taking out of their proper congenital environment. They commence to die off if kept out of that inherent environment. For example, whenever a child disobeys his parents, that child begins to die off and eventually dies, if left in that state (see, Ephesians 6: 1-3).Whenever intimate relationships are taking out of its proper environment that relationship will begin to die off. When a fish is taking out of the water, the organism will begin to die off-it's not dead, yet it's dying. Evidence of them all dying is that they will all be suffering in the state. Suffering means different things in different languages. I will show you throughout this book what I mean by this.

A perfect example is an intimate relationship that has present abuse, cheating, child custody hearings, and divorce court. That relationship is suffering and dying off because of the wrong elements being present. That relationship is in the wrong environment.

This book is centered on relationships: in the work place, business field, in intimate relationships, and between friends and parents and their children.

I really believe that relationships were originally designed by God to function where pain, hurt and crying are exempt. I believe if I make the choice to lie to you. I can make that same decision not to. I will get a little deeper. If I make the ultimate decision to cheat on you, I can make the same decision not to cheat on you. If I choose to abuse you in any form, I can make the decision not to. You still have the will to choose what to do. What will you do?

This is why I believe that relationships don't fail, but people do. People fail to execute the divine principles set forth by God to make their relationship last until death due them apart.

In intimate relationships, pain, hurt and crying comes as a result of the wrong elements being present and the right ones rejected. Whenever someone falls out of love with their mate, their focus and will has changed. The first moments you had before sex, when all you thought about was her, are no more. Now you have another focus and desire. You have present elements of destruction. These will eventually destroy the relationship-Because you are no longer single minded.

This book will reveal the right principles on how to fall back in love with them and how to never fall out of love with them. The relationship can always be as it started. This is only realized when the relationship is in the right principle environment. This book also deals with the difference between the woman and the lady, the man and the gentlemen, the destructive force of playing games, and also how to properly train your child in the way they should go.

This book will also reveal the difference between half trusts, half dedication, half sacrifice, half communication, and much more. And when operating in them completely, the practice will cause your relationships to last until death due the two apart.

Moreover, this is not a work of fiction. People are dying and hurting and need real answers to their real problems.

The authority behind this book is the bible, psychologist's view as well as my very own personal experience. You will see as you read it that there will sometimes be psychology verses the bible. As a student of law, whenever a law passes that contradicts the United States

Constitutions, that same law is said to be unconstitutional. This law has to change. So whenever you have a psychologist's view that conflicts with the word of God, you must change that view. Remember that God deals with the body, soul and spirit. Psychology deals with the mind. Remember this, because your eternal soul is on the line.

I don't profess to know everything. I am only doing my part in the building of a great people for the will of God.

I spent many years writing and rewriting this book. I can recall many times I wanted to just give up and die because of what I was going through. I reveal some of the things in this book as well as the second part of this book. That book is entitled, the other side of me, notwithstanding, I reveal all in the two part book of my life. This book is entitled once an outcast to society, but now destines to eventually become the greatest talent ever. These projects are all written by me along with their movie scripts and unproduced original soundtrack lyrics.

This Future Prospect series which consist of two books, two movies, two soundtracks as well as a family sitcom, I believe will reach hundreds of millions of people worldwide.

In conclusion, the first part of this book rebuts the wrong lifestyle of the man and the woman. And it positions them to take a stand to either be the lady or the gentlemen. I believe then they should enter that relationship. Because now they can be equip to sustain their relationship.

DEDICATION:

I dedicate this book to my beautiful fiancée Aisha Rene White, and all who believed in me from the start.

Special dedications to all who truly desire to live in a lasting relationship until you leave this earth. This series will truly aid you in that desire. And honor to my older sister Keasha Damond and my mother Gilda Damond who always is there for me.

DEDICATION: (PART 2)

I would like to dedicate this book to all my mentors: Finis Jennings Dake, Verna Bradley Jackson & Tommy Jackson, (My Second Set Of Parents), Pastor George J, & Wife Evette J (My Other Parents), Big Lloyd, Pastor Eric Mathews, Pastor Rene Thomas, Pastor G Craig Lewis, Pastor John Hagee, Pastor Rod Parsley, My Best Friend Cheryl Brown, Pastor M. Stone. You all truly played great roles in my life. I thank God for you all.

PART ONE

Which one are you in?

I believe if a man is not a gentleman and a woman is not a lady. Their intimate relationship will suffer a lot of unnecessary ups and downs. They will have to endure a lot of emotional and physical pains.

Written by Glenn Calvin Damond

©2014 by Glenn C. Damond

CHAPTER 1: THE WOMAN AND THE LADY

(Which one are you?)

This chapter can be used to assist women in evolving into a lady. I believe there is a great difference between being a woman and being a lady. A woman reaches womanhood based upon a certain age, preferably 20. Nevertheless, a lady on the other hand, is a woman who exhibits appropriate mannerisms. This book will deal with this issue concisely, for it is only a prelude in comparison to part two of this book, "The other side of me". This deals exclusively with the issue. This book is written for the man and the woman, the head of the household, and his help mate. I know it starts with them. They have to get ready to bring the family back in order, and become the powerhouses in the earth. It's time to take the family back out of the hand of the devil and the state systems. Let's get started.

Women are not naturally embedded with the qualities of a lady. They have to be trained in that area of life. Culturally speaking, we become products of our environment. The mileu I'm speaking about is more potent and closely knitted together then the neighborhood we call our home. The first thought that pops into the human mind when speaking about their environment, is their house or place they reside in.

Contrary to common belief, your environment is truly something that surrounds you. It is all the conditions, circumstances, and influences surrounding, and affecting the development of, an organism or group of organisms.

Remember the cover of this book; whenever an organism steps outside of its proper environment, they start to die off.

So in essence, your environment could be second hand smoke. When you live in the environment of second hand smoke, you could get lung cancer (see, wells, 1998), heart disease(see, Howard et al., 1998), and breast cancer in women (see, Lash & Aschengrau, 1994). This will make you becoming of an organism dying off.

Women that are not train in how to become a lady usually allow their teaching to stem from different sources. These sources can be from anywhere from a song, a book, TV show or even a motion picture. This source could be whatever or whoever you consider for your guidance. The true test to prove if these sources are worthy to continue to govern your life by, is to consider the outcome. After obeying their instructions, did your life become that of pain, hurt, or crying? I believe if the source produced true peace, this is a good one.

When I followed the guidance in that song, did it cause my relationship to suffer in any way what so ever? When I watched that favorite motion picture, following the script, did I get away with robbing the bank? When I listened to what the rapper said about how to treat my woman, did she, being a good woman, accept that lifestyle?

What about that talk show, when I obeyed the instruction of that talk show host, about dishonoring and rejecting Jesus, did my life become greater in peace ?Or am I successful and miserable ? What about that favorite song that is informing me to use sex as a weapon? Wouldn't I destroy my goods and become a neighborhood sex toy-at the same time be miserable inside.

The message in the song became the environment whereby I governed my life. I have allowed that song to be my source of truth. In doing so my source of truth caused me to have problems in my relationship.

And I accepted those problems because my source of truth told also told me that all men cheat, just make sure that he brings the pay check home and takes care of the home.

The source of truth told me as long my man comes home to me at night, it doesn't matter what he does in the street. I will be alright with that. If this is the case, then my source of truth is the wrong environment to live in. This source is producing a negative result, for it is destroying my life-and wounding my heart and mind extremely bad.

So what are you saying Mr. Damond? Am I a bad person? I will not say that. I will say that the individual was just taught the wrong principles to govern their lives by. In the second part of this book, on the front cover, I have the following message, "An organism without proper guidance is the epitome of destruction." So do you see where I am going with this?

A person can have a good heart, yet be taught the wrong principles to live by. So I'm not saying that that person is bad. What would make them bad is if after they have received good sound teaching or instructions, notwithstanding, they still refuse to live by them. For example, I know selling drugs is bad, but I am doing it to provide for my family. So now I am justifying being a bad person.

You say that companies will not hire you for being a convicted felon. I am a living witness that you can make it. I was convicted of 3 felonies and spent 18 years in prison. I have been going in and out of prison since I was a teenager. Yet in 16 months I had 6 different jobs, that is 4 restaurant jobs (apple bees, Joes crab shack, Chili's and BJs restaurant), a car wash job and a cleaning job. So you can make it as a convicted felon.

Therefore, living right can be done as well as obtaining a nice job. In this situation, good instructions will be to get a good job and stay free to be there for your family. A person, who refuses this sound teaching and continues to sell drugs destroying a community, will be considered a bad person.

I understand that life. You already know that I grew up in the war zone, New Orleans. At this time, the city made the murder capital twice. I am not glorifying that. I am simple trying to show you that what you did. I have been there. I sold cocaine, marijuana, and heroin-plus I was using all three with the addition of drinking. Now you can't pay me to smoke a cigarette. I am doing something good with my life. And I am proud of myself. You can do the same with your life. I am a great example of how God can take one who endangered society and change him to a blessing for society.

I will now talk more about the word environment.

ENVIRONMENT: A surrounding or being surrounded. Something that surrounds; surroundings. All conditions, circumstances, and influences surrounding, and affecting the development of, an organism or group of organisms.

Now let's look at the word circumstances.

CIRCUMSTANCE: A fact or events accompany another, either incidentally or as an essential condition or determining factor. Any happening or fact; event. Conditions surrounding and affecting a person.

The title of this part asks women, which one are you in, the woman or the lady. There is the possibility that the woman could be a lady, but she has to possess the qualities of a lady and govern her life by those same qualities.

When you finish reading this chapter you will be able to tell the difference between a woman and the lady, the whore and the lady. The divine principle says that you will know a person by what they do (see, Matthews 7:16 & 20). This principle is essential for selecting a woman you may want to spend the rest of your life with.

When you understand these principles that I am about to talk about in the few chapters, both good and bad, you will be able to make the right decision about the woman you want to marry. I must let you know that this first chapter deals with the bad woman, the whore, the one who will destroy your life. This chapter is not to suggest that women who possess the attributes of a whore cannot change. Some will never change, yet others do.

I was a man-whore as a teen and well off into adulthood. Notwithstanding, look at me now in 2013 – I am in the process of building lives for the bettering of humanity as a whole.

Now let's go back to the word environment. When I first started writing this chapter, I said the environment that I was speaking about is more potent and closely knitted together. This is more closely knitted together than the neighborhood that you lay your head i.e. young girl's environment can be her older sister.

Let's get deeper!

Picture the scenery! The 21 year old sister lounges in her younger sister's room styling her hair. So this process is taking place, the older sister might commence to advice the younger sister about her relationship with young men. She might say something around the following lines." Lil sis, you have to keep them young boys on the edge and make them beg for your sex for a sense of control. You have to take them for everything they have. Do not just sleep with them for free; make them pay for it some kind of way? You have to control the relationship."

The younger sister listens prudently. I mean after all, this is big sister. She loves me and would never tell me anything wrong, especially something whereby I might hurt myself.

What the younger sister does not realize is that her older sister is only informing her about the ways she may have been conducting her relationship and other things she strongly feels good about. Also, she does not understand that it is not a good deal to have 3 or 4 baby daddies like big sister. And the one she is pregnant with now is another baby daddy. The younger sister does not see that that is four relationships that didn't work.

The divine principle says that it is not good to have children by all those different men. (See, Proverbs 5: 15-17).It is not good to try to control the man because you don't want to be hurt. As his wife, you must submit yourself to him. (See, Ephesians 5: 22). If you operate in any other manner, you are out of the divine plan of God. You will be hurt spiritually and mentally, maybe even physically.

This is essential to the young girl because the environment that she is living in is destroying her relationships and life. Her sister may mean good by her, but you have to keep in mind she is only speaking about what she knows as truth.

This is her truth.

This truth eventually becomes the little girl's environment. This is the influences that are affecting her growth as a woman. She will eventually evolve into an immoral woman instead of a lady. She is taught by the environment to have sex at a young age. She is then to make a little teen age boy beg for her sex-she is 14 years old. This environment spells destruction. This is the atmosphere of pain, hurt and crying. When it is all said and done, when the world is finish with this little girl, she could become a nightmare to many men.

The reason is because that environment will scar her for life. It could cause her to feel lower than dirt. If this happens, when she begins to feel this way, her life will become one without restraints. She will begin to do any immoral act that comes to mind. A tragic situation! That same teenage girl could have received the right instruction and lived a better life.

This is the true essence of the second part of this book, The other side of me; on the front cover of the book are the words, "An organism without proper guidance is the epitome of destruction. " I really need you to see this in her life.

A GOOD EXAMPLE OF THIS TEACHING

Let's say that this little girl's boyfriend approaches her about having sex with her that they been having. She listens to the advice of her sister and refuses him this time. The teen goes out and have sex with another teenager girl. The other teen finds out (his girlfriend) and is hurt (scared) by it. She then goes out to get even by having sex with another teen boy-one she knows been had a crush on her/. She acts off emotions.

I had one woman tell me that she doesn't get mad or upset if a man cheats on her. She gets even. He cheats then I do the same.

Now what if this person that she is having sex with has a STD? The girl is not thinking logic, only about getting even. She is hurting. Hurt people hurt people and further hurt themselves in the process. Now she is pregnant with a STD. Do you see where I am going with this?

Again, refer back to the surtitle of the second part, an organism without proper guidance is the epitome of destruction." That one piece of advice can cause you a life time of pain.

The proper environment for the girl says not to refuse your mate for sex unless the both of you come together and agree. But this speaks to the married couple-which the girl should become before she has sex in the first place. (1 Corinthians 7:4 & 5).This is the principles that will help the little girl evolve into a lady. This is her true environment that will spell true peace and happiness until death due the two apart. This is the conditions that should be affecting the girl.

ANOTHER GOOD EXAMPLE IS

Now taking female's favorite R/B singer that she loves so dearly. She buys all of her CDs. This singer in time becomes the girl's truth-her environment. This artist music becomes the young girl influences that affect the way she deals with her relationships. It maybe the teaching her how to let the man abuse her. That message may say to allow him to run wild in the streets with his friends. Then when he comes home make love to.

What kind of message is that? I will tell you. It is one that tells me as a man, I can do what I want to do with other women. This is because you will be home when I get there to give me more sex.

I remember the female name Jay who I wanted me to fall in love with. I really was feeling her, really though. She is a beautiful woman. I asked her one day that if me and her were together and another woman passed. And I stared at this other woman as if she wasn't there. What would she do? She told me that men will be men as long as I respect her.

Now what she is telling me is that her environment taught her to allow men to cheat on her-just don't do it around her, because all men cheat. She was in a relationship at the time and she said it was not serious. She was looking for something solid. She was entertaining me on the same level.

I could tell from dealing with her that she wanted to be in a relationship where she controlled the man and the relationship. That wasn't happening with me- my mind is too strong. I know my place as the head of the home. She desired this position because she didn't want to get hurt anymore.

This is an area where a lot of women fail. This is because the man is designed to protect you mentally, spiritually and physically. When they have to do it themselves it means an organism is out of order.

Jay was not use to dealing with my kind. She knew she had to come correct when dealing with me. As a result, she begins to act shy when I approached her to talk to her. She would sometimes avoid eye contact with me because I was able to read her.

I still like her. She has evolved into a woman without lady qualities. She entertained me and two of mine friends at the same time on the relationship level. We didn't care we were bosses and had the chicks who everybody wanted.

Her environment taught her this. As a result she was always stressed out. Her environment produced stress.

Stress is an improper environment to live in because it can cause lower back pain (Lamp et al., 1998). Stress can cause the development of genital herpes (VanderPlate, Aral, & Magder, 1988), and periodontal disease (Marcenes & Sheiham, 1992). It is sad to say, but this female eventually contracted the STD- **HERPES.**

This is a very beautiful female and she has a kind heart. She just been hurt and abused so much that it's hard for her to trust anyone. So she plays with men heart because she is hurting and she wants someone to feel her pain. She suffers from pass repression. At this stage in her life it's not good for men to get in a relationship with her. She can be a good friend- she is. That pain has to get out of her to have a truly great intimate relationship.

The environment she governs her life by is destroying her. She has sex with a lot of different men. This takes away her value to be a lady. She likes to sell her body to take care of her son. This is her excuse for the prostitution lifestyle.

Her actions will stop her from being with a good man. I believe a good man won't be able to trust her. She told me she wanted a godly man. I told her that a godly man has certain standards he wants in a woman. I believe she said this because she wants a man that will accept her pass and one who will not cheat on her.

THE FOOLISH WOMAN

When I say foolish, I mean the woman who lacks the qualities of being a lady. Remember, women govern their lives by what their environment teaches them if they accepted that environment as truth. So this doesn't make them a bad person. They are just acting out what they received as truth. As explained earlier, I told you what makes them a bad person. This still doesn't make them right or what they are doing right. I am just helping you understand the situation.

Let's look closely at the word foolish.

Foolish: without good sense or wisdom; silly, unwise. Ridiculous; absurd. Abashed; embarrassed. Worthless.

Now let's look at the following words: silly, unwise, worthless. These words depict the foolish woman. The one society deems as a whore, or a slut. This woman as you will see would mentally destroy a good man.

Now let's look closely at the words.

Silly: simple; plain; innocent, feeble; infirm; helpless. Feebleminded; imbecile. Having or showing little sense, judgment, or sobriety; foolish, stupid.

Before I go on, I would like to say. That the reason I am defining all of these words. Is because in them and as I go on, you will see the difference between the woman and the lady. When I start describing the lady, you will see the total difference.

Unwise: having or showing a lack of wisdom or sound judgment; foolish.

Worthless: without worth or merit; useless, valueless.

The woman who lacks the qualities of a lady possesses the qualities of a foolish woman. This means she doesn't use common sense. She is simple minded. Which means you can deceive her easily. She believes a lot of what evidence cannot produce as truth. She has a weak mind. She doesn't have standards of truth. You could dictate her life by what you say.

She has bad judgment. Which means her decisions are poor? She has a problem discerning who means her good and who doesn't .She is worthless, useless and valueless. She will bring you nothing but pain, heartache, hurt, stress and disappointment. I am a living witness of this.

MORE ATTRIBUTES

1. She is clamorous. (See, Proverbs 9: 13; 7:11)." A foolish woman is clamorous:" The Greek text translates the word clamorous, "haw-maw" and it means to make a loud sound. To be in great commotion or tumult, to rage, roar, sound be troubled, be in an uproar.

She is boisterous. This means she is unmannerly, violent, unruly, crude, and coarse. She is in uproar. Which means she likes to stir up violence or commotion? She is messy. She is outspoken in a nasty and perverted manner.

Her coarse actions are shown when she verbally abuses someone instead of gently talking to them.

2. She knows nothing (Pr.9:13). This means she knows no shame. She is ignorant and depraved. She shows no shame when she sells her body for money. When she does all type of perverted things for money – knowing she has a man at home. She is depraved. She loves to lead others into wrong evil habits. She helps to make them morally bad, corrupt and perverted.

This is the attributes of the immoral woman. She takes the man that is willing to be good to her and missuses him. Her goal is to break him and make him weak for her. That way she could keep him there with her for security and at the same time run wild with other men in the streets.

This woman is not shamed when she allows a man to sex her in the car, on the car or on the porch or even in the pool.

She feels good letting a man sex her on the job for a few dollars while her boyfriend or husband is at home.

She feels no shame when she jerks a man off while driving down the street or in a club, even sitting on the porch.

3. She watches for men to seduce(Pr.9:14) This means she looks for men she think is weak or knows is weak and tries to seduce them for her own pleasure.

Her pleasure may be for sexual reasons. Or to pass time like women who work in prison systems do. (See verses-15, 16, & 17).

She paints the picture that what she has is good and not worth passing up. This she does to make the temptation stronger.

Reasons to stay away from her

1. She are deceptive

When she speaks. Most of the time is to get something out of you. Her motives are 95% of the times impure. They are selfish. She is lying to get something from the man. (Pr.5:3) I'm a witness of this.

2. She is a flatterer (Pr.5:3)

This means she will say what she has to say only to get what she needs to get out of you at that moment. She will smooth talk you. If she has to talk about how good you look, how sexy you walk, or how sweet you talk. When you give your ear to her to the point where she has your attention she has accomplished her goal. Which was to get in your head?

Now all she has to do is make it seem like she will let you touch her. Then she feels like she could get anything out of you. Or get you to do anything.

She will sway you with her sincere talk, she will make her face look as friendly and sincere as she can (Pr.7:13). She may touch you to let you know that she is willing to go farther to get what she wants or needs at that time (Pr.7:12). She is bold with her saying because she knows no shame (v13). Her motives are hidden (v 10). She will make her words irresistible to cause you to yield to her will (Pr.7:21).

3. She is stubborn (Pr.7:11)

This means she is stuck in her immoral ways. Her ways become the guiding force of her life. These same ways are causing her to live in pain, hurt, stress, and to suffer.

4. She runs wild in the streets (Pro.7:11, 12)

This means she hangs out in clubs all night destroying herself with alcohol "(Maok& Anton, 1999; wood et al, 2001).

The short-term risks and problems alcohol produces dizziness, nausea, and vomiting.

The long term health effects of heavy drinking are heart disease, hypertension, and stroke. Excessive drinking is also correlated with an elevated risk for various types of cancer, including oral, stomach, pancreatic, colon, and rectal cancer. Moreover, serious drinking problems can lead to cirrhosis of liver, malnutrition, pregnancy complications, brain damage, and neurological disorders.

Finally, alcoholism can produce severe psychotic states, characterized by delirium, disorientation, and characterized by delirium, disorientation, and hallucinations."

(Taken from psychology Applied to Modern life).
I talk more about the risk of alcohol in Chapter 4." Organisms dying off when they indulge in desired habits. In the second part of this book.

The loose women like to run the street and attend every social gathering where they can dress to tease men (Pr.7:10). They walk with short steps with seductive clothes on with their necks stretched forth, moving their bodies to attract the attention of men (Isa.3:16) Wearing thons.

They do this on the street corner, at the club, at the mall, game, etc, when they have a man at home already.

These women are very dangerous. They don't care. . They just gloat over making men fall weak for them. It's a game to them.

5. She is unpredictable (Pr.5:6)

This means she constantly changes her tricks to keep your attention. When she feels she has captured you. Then there is no more she needs to do. Now she knows you will chase her.

When you show you are not interested in her no more she then will feel like she has lost control. Then she will do whatever is possible to gain your attention back.

Once you feel you figured her out, she will change on you to keep you off balance and confused. She will change the way she dresses, talk, and act, all to keep you chasing her.

6. She will ruin your reputation (v.9)

Maybe you are a man of God and get caught with a loose woman. This could ruin your effect on lives.

She will cause you years of trouble. You will constantly get into conflicts with other men over her. She knows all she has to do is cry to you after she messes up and she has you right back where she had you.

Then she will go and tease another man for more attention until you find that out. Then she will cry and plead how much she needs you, put the sex on you. Then you're right back where she had you again.

(v.9:10) This could mean after you have had sexually dealings with her for a while. Then you decide to not have any farther dealings with her for whatever reason. Which will make her upset in which a immoral woman hates and can't accept rejection. This can turn out good at first because she may follow you around to see what is the problem.

She will see that you don't want to have any farther dealings with her. She might then, like in today's world, put a sex charge on you. The plot maybe to allow you to win in criminal court, but loses in civil court.

She then receives your money. Her secret lover then will be filled with your money. Some will marry you to cover their plan. Then when they divorce you. Then depart with half of what you work many years to establish. The bible says it this way. "Lest strangers be filled with thy wealth; and thy labors be in the house of a stranger;" (V.10)

7. She will bring substance demolition (Pr.5:18)

I see a lot of this in Hollywood. I know it doesn't always be the women's fault. I do know women pursue men because they have riches. They will stay with them, marry them, the create conflict to divorce them.

Today the law is made where you have to continue to take care of them and the children. They don't think about that you never had a problem with taking care of your children. She wants it like this so all the money could come through her hands. That way she could enjoy it with the man you never knew about. She had to keep that from you because the law also says if you could prove she was unfaithful. Then she gets nothing. But she keeps this from you. Now sit back and watch how quick they get married, enjoy houses, cars, money and land –then make it where you can only see your children at a certain time and day.

Listen to the bible. "Lest strangers be filled with thy wealth; and thy labors be in the house of a stranger."

Pg.30

And you still think this is a game. You better wake up and open your eyes. A immoral woman will change some of her ways to make you feel like she is trying to change. This is only because her motives are selfish and she hasn't gotten anything out of you yet. She hasn't put herself in the position where you have to take care of her yet.

She may reach this level. Then all you have to do is make her mad. Then she will do what she knows will hurt you. This shows her lack of integrity. You could refuse to do something or give her something.

Then she will go out to one of her secret lovers, sex him, maybe just touch him or make him think he will get something out of her. Then get what she wants. Then come home flashings it in your face. Then when the argument starts she will tell you her friend gave it to her and if you would have. She wouldn't have had to go in the streets and get it.

8. She will bring diseases home (Pr.5:11)

This is critical because she could bring home herpes or HIV. This is something you can't get rid of apart from God. "And thou mourn (to growl) at the last, when thy flesh. And thy body is consumed. I know when your body is consumed. It ceases to be. The disease has accomplished its mission which was to destroy you. This is the danger in lying with a foolish woman.

9. She will ruin the good man (Pr.5:14)

I was at this point before when I was hurt by this foolish woman. The first woman I fell in lust with. I was thinking about so many evil things to do to her that I won't even mention them. I grew up a ganasta. I changed my life by God's grace. I really wanted to love this female with all my heart and treat her like she never had been treated. So when she hurt me. I was going to destroy her and everyone she loved. This was because of her immature whorish ways.

I always fell for the foolish women.

This woman begins to spread rumors about me, all of which were lies. I was going too literally hurt this person, but I shook back and realized. That she is not worth it because she is nothing. She is worthless.

10. She will bring regret (Pr.5:12, 13)

This is because your friends told you about this female. Your family told you about her and you still wanted to have her.

This was me in regards to the first woman I fell in lust with. My friend told me "man she is an immoral woman. She brought a dress to go out just so she could get lucky and have sex with one of the local rappers who was coming in town. My friend told her that the rapper had a girl. She said he might bring someone with him.

My little brother told me that I am down bad chasing after nothing .My other friend Arthur who had hooked me up with her told me to leave her alone. She is a slut. You are about to be a great. She is nothing.I didn't listen. The result was I regret I ever fell in lust with that person.

11. Her end is death (Pr.5:4, 5)

She can give you a disease that will ruin your life. She can put you in a conflict that can cause your death.

If you follow her, she can destroy everything about you (Pr.2:19), She forsakes godly parental guidance (v.17). She renounces godly principles. She shortens her life by the lifestyle she lives (v.18). She destroys men unmercifully and ruins them permanently (v.19).

This is the immoral, the foolish woman. This is the one who lacks the qualities of a lady.

Men could just walk up to her and touch her body in an improper way if or if she doesn't have a man at home. Men can disrespect her and nothing will be done about it.

She is an organism dying off. One that needs to change her ways with the help of God before she closes her eyes and wake up in eternal pain, regret, and suffering . She will enter a place where she won't find a place, or area, or resting place from pain where she could stop and take a break one second. (Pr.5:5) (Rev.14:11). "And they have no rest day nor night"

Now keep reading, part 2 will show you the lady, the virtuous woman. I know this is the one to be cherishing the rest of her life.

Chapter 2: The woman and the Lady? (Part 2)

(Which one are you?)

"Who can find a virtuous woman? For her price is far above rubies. (Pr. 31:10)"

This is the women with the qualities of a lady. She is strong in all moral and mental qualities. (Pr. 12:4)

Thank God for the lady. This is the one who you will never have to worry about cheating on you or hurting you. The one you better commit your all to and never leave her.

Let's look at the word "Lady"

Lady = the mistress of a household; now obsolete except in the phrase the lady of the house. A woman who has the rights, rule, or authority of a lord. A woman who is of high social position, who's also polite, refined, and well mannered.

This is the lady. The mistress in the manner of the woman in control. This is the dame woman. The virtuous woman. The woman who is to be praised above money.

The difference between the woman and the lady lays within mannerisms they both exhibit. The previous chapter showed you the ways of the woman without qualities of a lady. This chapter will dive into the qualities of the lady.

This is the organism that is in her proper environment. Therefore she lives in peace, prospers in the body, soul and mind and she enjoys the longevity of life.

The lady is well mannered, considerate with high standards of proper behavior, this means she sits in a proper way rather eating or just lounging. She crosses her legs or closes them so that she doesn't give men the wrong impression of her.

She knows how each eating utensil is to be set on the table. She speaks a certain way. She treats people the right way. She allows her husband to sex her in the proper way and not in a perverted way. Now let's get deeper into her ways. The proper environment for women to live in.

1. She is morally developed (Pr. 31:10)

This means she is strong in all morals and mental qualities. This lady's ways are right toward everyone. She is not swayed by public opinions. She receives instructions from people, but values only what she knows is good.

The sayings of a close friend don't always govern her life. She understands that people sometimes have hidden agendas. People's opinions don't dictate her way of life or how she treats and deals with her relationships with others. She knows that this independent mentally. So she makes her decisions in life based on divine truths and not on other people's feelings.

2. She can be trusted (v. 11, 12)

This is in regards to her mate. Her mate completely trusts her not to sleep with another man. He isn't over protected of her. He doesn't get jealous because he knows to sleep with another man is beneath her.

The lady despises this with all of her heart. She honors her body too much and would never participate in such a thing- not even in her weakness hour. She only lies with her husband. She only wants to spend the rest of her life with one man.

She doesn't dangle other men just in case it doesn't work between her and her mate.

She isn't quick to get into a serious relationship until she knows in heart that it will be sealed until death does them apart.

Her husband trusts her to not allow her beauty and much attention from men to cause her to become egoistic. So that she begin to put men through emotional ego trips- catering to their egos. When in actuality she is not really interested in them.

She doesn't lead men on. She is straight forward with them, letting them know that she has a man. This all has to do with him having total confidence in her integrity, ability and her good character. He trusts her never to lie to him or anyone for that matter. She does him good all the days of his life and never evil.

She never deceives him. She never hurts him. She never cheats on him in spite of common belief. She never puts into a situation where he could get hurt or killed. She never talks evil behind his back. The divine principle says that she does good and not evil all the days of his life (v.12). This is the lady and the proper environment that she lives in.

Her husband trusts her to handle business matters. He trusts her with their child, with their money. He trusts her to feed him physically and mentally. He also trusts her with his life because she will do him good all the days of his life.

3. She is skillful and ready to work (v.13)

She seeks wool and flax which means that she is skillful in creating or devising. She learns if she doesn't know a given art or skill. She learns the right way because she is proficient.

She works willing with her hands. This means a job. There is nothing wrong with having a job. Everyone can't be C.E.Os., or Entrepreneurs. There has to be labors.

4. She is business minded (v.14, 16, 18, 24)

Verse 14 says the lady is like the merchant's ships. Which means she imports and exports goods? She takes in enough to sell and keep some for her family.

Verse 16 says she invest to supply for her growing family. She does what is necessary to learn of a business on an education level. Then she invests in it because she understands the value in being independent.

True Independence

True independence means that she is free from the influence, guidance, or control of another or others.

Take women who have been emotionally hurt. She can't wait on the right man to come along and think all of her wombs will be healed. She has to understand that self means the total, essential, or particular being of a person.

She is whole when she is whole within herself. She must release whatever pain or hurt she feeling and move on. If she waits on a man to make her whole she becomes co-dependent.

This is not to say that she doesn't have to have a man. They both have to learn to be independent of the other. That way if one was to live, death speaking, the other won't give up on life.

Verse 18 says that she is honest in her business dealings. This means when she makes a contract. The contract isn't written up to get over on anyone. In any business deal she makes, she does it the right way.

Verse 24 seems to depict what I believe a clothing line because she makes clothes and sell them. While verse 16 leaves it open to venture into any business field.It all spells that she is business minded.

5. She's a cook (v.15)

This means she cooks for her household. It's also revealed in that verse that she has a maiden. Which means it's not wrong for someone to have a maid. It's a job. They need work too. The woman might be able to cook at times, but it's possible that she has a busy schedule where she's not able to. This is where the maid comes in at.

This doesn't mean that the woman who can't cook is evil. Rather it should be an incentive for her to learn the craft of cooking; Verse 17 says also that she supplies her family with food. This could mean buying it from the store and allowing the maid to cook it

Verse 21 reveals that she also clothes her family with necessary clothing for winter. She does her part to keep them warm, with food and healthy.

6. She is a giver (v.20)

This means she is not all about herself. She extends a helping hand to all need. She not only gives money or material things. She gives a smile, a helping hand and a good word.

7. She is a dresser (v. 22)

There is nothing wrong with looking and dressing good. This is an attribute of a lady. She doesn't dress in a way to attract the lusts of men.

8. Her husband is well respected (v.23, 25)

This is because she is lady and she is married to a gentleman.

He r husband is not only respected for his place of position in society, but also because his wife is reflection of him.

9. Her words are carefully selected (v.26)

This means she doesn't use profanity. Her vocabulary is filled with wise words to uplift someone never to tare them down. This also means she gives wise instructions on every level. This farther means that she is intelligent, and highly cultured mined and mannered. When she talks to people it's always with respect looking them eye to eye.

She speaks kind words to everyone she come in contact with. Foolish words are far from her.

10. She manages her household (v.27)

The first part of that verse means that she manages or helps manage the money to keep her household straight. The teachings that she receives she passes them on to her children to cause them to behave well and keep the right company.

She's teaches them the business field and God's ways of the business field. She teaches them godly living, and she helps them to be stable in mind, body and spirit.

The second part of the verse deals with responsibility. The lady teaches her children to be responsible by giving them chores to the benefit of the household as a whole, when they show faithfulness. She gives them more, but not more than they can handle.

She gives each of her children a chore and their proper food, clothing and allowance. She gives them the proper education knowing that it's a part of raising them.

She doesn't allow the streets or the state to raise her children. She educates them and protects them mentally, physically and spiritually from all danger.

11. <u>She stands out</u> (v.29, 30, and 31)
This means she is above other women in the motherhood, being a wife and God's own. She is a good decorator of the house.

12. <u>She submits to her husband</u> (Eph 5:22)
To submit to someone means to be obedient to them. Some women who been in relationship with a strong minded man who took advantage of them or maybe a man who use to beat them. They feel they have to have some kind of control to enter another relationship. Control leads to rebellion and resentment; killers in a relationship. It's about submitting to your husband.

Chapter 3. The man verses the Gentleman

I've just completed 2 chapters dealing with the woman and the lady. Now it's time to deal with me, the man verses the gentleman. In this day in time, homes are out of order, and part of the reason for this is because the man is out of order. Men are ignorant to the truth on how to govern their homes and what is a man's position in society.

One reason for this is because we are not naturally embedded with the qualities to be a gentleman. Another reason is due to the administration we were raised up under. I like to use the psychologist's theory that, over time, organisms originate and become adapted to their environment by biological means.

Let me give you two examples. Take a child whose parents raised him to be racial. When he is developed in life (this is to say someone doesn't show him the right way) his life will be governed like that- hating another race of people.

Take the ghetto child, in the ghetto. When we give birth to children (speaking of the women) majority of the time it's a by a female we met in the club, hood, school or even on the job. Which means she is a part of our environment? So nine times out of ten, we are exposed to same rules whereby we raise our child.

Let's get deeper.

Couples in the ghetto don't always last. This is because if we are not able to raise our child properly. It is due to our lack of being gentlemen. That is to be a gentleman you have……

to be equipped with the qualities that is becoming of a gentleman. Raising a child properly is one of those qualities.

Now since couples don't last that long because pregnancy might result by a mistake of some kind. It could have been the two of you were so intoxicated with alcohol that you didn't protect yourself. So due to this we have to separate our times with the child because we live in two different homes and have different friends. As a father, when it is my time to watch the child I bring him around my friends, these are thugs. The nature of the thug exposes them to drugs, profanity, and violence.

Another trend that takes place is the exposer to inappropriate behavior. At a very early age we are amused when we see two four year old children kissing. We expose them to all of this at a very early age and when they grow up like this. We sit back and wonder where we went wrong. We don't understand that the child has become a product of what we exposed them to. Hence the terms biological evolution .The truth of the matter is that we don't most of the time know that we are in the wrong. We are only being what we know to be and doing what we believe is right.\

Now let's get into what psychologist say about the role of man. Then we will get into what God says. The following is taken from the book, "psychology Applied to Modern life."

Role Expectation for males

"A number of psychologists have sought to pinpoint the essence of the traditional male role (Brannon, 1976, Levant, 1996; Pleck, 1995).Many consider antifemininity to be the central theme that runs through the male gender role. That is, "real men shouldn't act in any way that might be perceived as feminine.

For example, men should not publicly display vulnerable emotions, should avoid feminine occupations, and should not show obvious interest in relationships-especially homosexual ones. Five key attributes constitute the traditional male role (Brannon, 1976; Jansz, 2000). Achievement to prove their masculinity, men need to beat out other men at work and at sports.

Having a high-status job, driving an expensive car. And making lots of money aspects of this element.

Aggression: Men should be tough and fight for what they believe is right. They should aggressively defend themselves and those they love against threats.

Autonomy: Men should be self-reliant and not admit to being dependent on others.

Sexuality: real men are heterosexual and are highly motivated to pursue sexual activities and conquests.

Stoicism: Men should not share their pain or express their "soft" feelings, they should be cool and calm under pressure.

Gender- role expectations for males have remained relatively stable for years. However, the male role may be undergoing some changes. According to Joseph pleck (1995), who has written extensively on this issue, in the traditional male role, masculinity, is validated by individual physical strength, aggressiveness, and emotional inexpressiveness.

In the Modern male role, masculinity is validated by economic achievement, organizational power, emotional control (even over anger), and emotional sensitivity and self-expression, but only with women.

Thus, in Modern societies, the traditional male role co-exists with some new expectations. Some theorists are using the plural "masculinities" to describe these variations in the male gender role (Connell, 1995; I. Harris, 1995). This flux role in expectations means that males are experiencing role inconsistencies and pressures to behave in ways that conflict with traditional masculinity: to communicate personal feelings, to nurture children and share in housework, to integrate sexuality with love, and to curb aggression(levantt,1996).

Some psychologists believe that these pressures have shaken traditional masculine norms sufficiently that mean men are experiencing a masculinity crisis (Levant, 1996). That is, they are feeling bewildered and confused, and their pride in being a man has been diminished.

Pressure to succeed

Most men are socialized to believe that job success is everything they are encouraged to be highly competitive and are taught that a man's masculinity is measured by the size of his paycheck and job status. As Christopher Kilmartin (2000) notes," There is always another man who has more money, higher status, a more attractive partner, or a bigger house. The traditional man…….must constantly work harder and faster."

Now God's view.

History

God's story is that the man was originally created to be the head, ruler, protector, and supplier. He is to be fruitful, to replenish, Nourish, cleave to woman, love her unconditionally, the blesser of his home, etc. This is all made up in the Gentleman.

Man has deviated from becoming this gentleman. The man, equipped with the qualities of the gentleman is supposed to be the powerhouse in the world with his help mate by his side. If the man isn't at home, then the house can be out of order. If he's home and doesn't understand his role, everything starts to go downhill. The children are then raised by the streets, and state-becoming products of their exposed environment. Then you have men at home, but lust (longing uncontrolled desires) has taken control of them. They don't exercise self-control in the sex bed, this is why and when they begin to touch their sons and daughters in a sexual manner. They begin to seek sexual experiences from outside the home also.

Psychologists teach us that rape is motivated from anger or someone wanting power. It may lead to that, but the real motivation behind it is lust that's out of control. What this means is that your sex drive is out of control?

We say today that he or she is out her body. We use to say that they were freaks. The professional way is to say that this person is a nymphomaniac, speaking of the woman. The truth of the matter is we always leave God out of our lives. This is the reason why our problems never get solved.

The good news is if you are still alive and able to read and understand this book. Then you can turn it around right now and become the man you are supposed to be. Not the man who 21 years old, has a job, a car, a little hair on his chest, but lack the qualities of a gentleman. But the man who possess the qualities of a gentleman and governs his life by them. This is the man you are called to be. So let's take your rightful place in this earth.

Let's take a look at the word" Gentleman" what does it mean.

Gentleman: a man of gentle or noble birth or superior social position. A polite, gracious, or considerate man having high standards of propriety or correct behavior. A man of indendent means who does not or need not work. A man who considers manual labor to be beneath him a man.

A gentleman indeed is a man but to be a man with the status of a gentleman you have to have high standards of propriety or correct behavior. Yes I could be a man who got my girl pregnant, but when it's time to raise that child. I don't step up to the task. This is because I don't possess the qualities of a gentleman. Now let's get into this correct behavior of the gentleman.

1. **The Head**
   Webster defines the head as the uppermost or forward most part of the body of a vertebrate, containing the brain or principal ganglia and the eyes, ears, nose, mouth, and jaws. The seat of the faculty of reason: mind. Mental ability or aptitude, freedom of choice or of action. The foremost or leading position.

   The authority behind him being the head comes from God. The head of what though? The answer is the head of his home. This means that he is in leading position for his wife and children. If he can't rule his home, then civil or religious government is out of question. (1 Timothy 3:5).

If the is out of order, the house is out of order. As the head he must do the following things that will be becoming of the gentleman- or a man of God.

2. **Dress the home**

The authority behind this is God." And the Lord God took man, and put him into the Garden of Eden to dress it. (Genesis 2:15)."

The Hebrew translation for dress (taken from the Strong's comprehensive concordance of the bible) means to work (in any sense to serve, till.

Man's garden is his home. He is supposed to dress it. In this situation, man gives delegated authority to his wife to dress the material external while he dresses the internal.

The lady decorates the inside of the house while the gentleman works on the internal. I'm talking about the head doing what the head is supposed to do. If the woman is by his side, then she may take part in it.

Now let's look at two words.

Serve: To prepare and offer, to be a servant to, to be of assistance to or promote the interests of, to fight or do military duty for to honor and obey.

Till: to prepare (land) for raising of crops. (We are going to say that crops represent killer weeds. Now I will show you how the head serves and tills his family to prepare them for life.

The Woman

Considering the man has been with the woman for some time now. He basically knows what she knows and doesn't know. So considering, she is not equipped to be that lady. He takes her from the stage that lacks lady qualities and helps her reach that area in her life.

This is because he understands that it's vital for her to exhibit lady like attributes for their relationship to last as to should. This is until their relationship to last as it should be. Which is until death does the two apart in happiness in between. If she has come out of a hurting relationship, and feels that the next man who comes along may make her happy. This is where he could start from. Yes he makes her smile again, but he lets her know that you have to be happy within yourself first before you can be truly happy with someone else.

He teaches her the importance of releasing that pain and living free. He teaches her about self, self-esteem, and what true independence is verses co- dependent. He teaches her how to be a lady. Now if the woman knows and possess these qualities, then that's great. I know they have a lot of independent women in society, but not every woman is on this level. I have also met a lot of females who don't know the difference between being a woman and a lady.

Propelled toward Independence

If the woman has a self-esteem problem, the gentleman begins to dress his woman with the clothing of it. He instructs her on how to have an attitude of acceptance, approval, and respect toward herself. That it doesn't matter what anyone says about you.

What you say and know is what counts, He teaches her that she should never be ashamed to make a choice in life and there is nothing wrong with making a mistake. That she should not be ashamed of where she comes from. Also to separate a dream from reality, always understand her limitations. He teaches her about herself. Letting her know that she must be complete within herself and not wait for a man to make her whole. The reason he teaches her this, because he wants her to be independent.

I want to say something I believe God made the man and the woman to depend on each other. What I am trying to convey is the message that if someone isn't there for you. You don't give up on life.

Now, the gentleman helps her understand that true independence is self-governing, free from the influence, guidance, or control of another or others. He wants both parties involved to be independent where each can survive without the other, and be able to help the other.

The gentleman shows his girl how to be a lady.

Now after she is fully dressed with this ability and knowledge, then they can get together and teach the children. He could take the son and dress him mentally and spiritually for life. She can take the girl and do her the same. This is true love. Love holds no one back from the best to be.

They can get together and dress their home to prepare them for the world. They would let them know (their children) the importance of being responsible, keeping bad company, education, business, everything about relationship, drugs, prison, the family, everything they need to know to survive in this world, and how to avoid pitfalls.

This is what the head does. I'll l explain it more.

3. **Keep the home**

"And the Lord God took the man, and put him into the Garden of Eden to keep it (Genesis 2:15) The Hebrew meaning for keep is to hedge about (as with thorns) guard, to protect attend, preserve.

The head is supposed to protect his home from murderers, rapist, drug dealers, and men trying to get his wife, or anything that threatens his household in any form. This will preserve them.

4. **Dominate the earth**

This commandment is giving to the man and the woman by God. "And God blessed them, and God said unto them, be fruitful, and multiply, and replenish the earth, subdue it: and have dominion over the fish of the sea and over the fowl of the air, and over every living thing that moveth upon the earth (Genesis 1:28)

Some are doing this and some aren't. You dominate something when you have control of it. It could be land, a business, your home, a fish, etc. This is the position man and woman is suppose to be in.

5. Give unconditional Love

This love is to be given to his home as well as outsiders. When you fall in unconditional love with someone, you become them. What affects them affects you.

When you truly love someone, you'll never do anything purposely to hurt them. Because hurting them is hurting yourself. Pain and hurt only comes in any relationship as a result of falling out of love- always. This only is the result of when you lose interest in someone. This means you have deviated from your first mind, intend, will, desire, and focus; Love is a long exciting journey. That is the love of God and the love between a woman and a man. The parties involved in it have to keep it that way.

There is love in correction of your child .You don't punish them. You correct them with love behind it, always remembering that correction is only to better them. Unconditional means being without conditions or limitations. The gentleman really needs to exercise this when dealing with a woman or child. You may have a woman who is hard to deal with. Deal with them in this authority- unconditional love. When you do so, you have God backing you. It's his love. He will bring the right results.

Now you must understand that this kind of love is supernatural. I mean how many people you know love people they don't even know or can still love a person beyond what you that did.

This love can only be given to you by God (Romans 5:5) it's his love. You receive it when you make Jesus the Lord of your life (10:9). You then must devolope it by staying in union with God (1John 4:16)

It's made perfect in us when we do this (v.17) When we obey Gods word you allow love, his love to grow in you (2:5) you developed it by practicing it on others even when its hard (4:7,8,11) That love sacrifices(v.9,10).

6. **Cherish his household**

We have a direct command from God to cherish our wives as we would do ourselves (Ephesians 5:28, 29) When you cherish someone. You keep them fondly in mind. Fond means to express feelings of affection, tender, having a strong liking or affection. This is a powerful statement. When you hold someone dear and treat affectionately. That means you won't never hit your wife to control her, or when she does something you don't agree with. You must hold your child (children) dear. That means you don't molest them. It doesn't matter if they are step children. You must hold them dearly. Also, the same way you tell your wife how much you love and care for her. You must do this to your children as well. Let this principle always follow when you correct them. This is what the gentleman does. He has high standards of propriety and correct behavior.

7. **Become one with his household**

The man and the woman are to become one according to God (Ephesians 5:31).This is not bondage, for to become one is true freedom, and peace of mind. This is because you can be in an intimate relationship and never have to worry about being cheated on, beaten on, lied to, abused mentally or physically, hurt, disrespected, etc.,. This is true freedom and peace. Your mind and body can rest and not stress. This is accomplished when you become one mind, will and desires

This simply means to be in agreement with. You must be on the same accord with her and your children,

In regards to your children, you want to have a relationship with your child whereby they are able to come to you and talk about anything. If you refused them that free spirit open line of communication, they will turn to someone else to teach them. Whoever they are, they may teach them the wrong way of doing things. You are the gentleman, the head of your home. It is your job to know. You must then communication to your child the proper way about sex, relationship, love, obeying God, etc.

In conclusion, effective communication is crucial to the success of a marriage. The damaging role that poor communication can play was clearly demonstrated in a study of couples getting a divorce (cleek Pearson, 1985) in this study, communication difficulties were the most frequently cited problem among both husbands and wives

Chapter 4 The man verses the Gentleman (part 2)

Continuing on from the last chapter, I like to get into more effective ways of communicating with your child. The following is taken from psychological Applied to Modern life.

" Set high, but reasonable standards children should be expected to be have in a socially appropriate manner for their age and to do as well as they can in school and in other activities. I believe that parents that don't communicate to their children how much they expect from them. They are teaching them not to expect much from themselves. "This is consistence with the law of expectation that says that people will do what you expect of them". The preceded wasn't taken from the book, but the following is.

Stay alert for "good" behavior and reward it. Most parents pay attention to children when they are misbehaving and ignore them when they're being good. This approach is backward! Develop the habit of praising good behavior so a child knows what you want.

Explain your reason when you ask a child to do something. Don't assume that a child can read your mind. Explaining the purpose of request can transform what might appear to be an arbitrary request into a reasonable one. It also encourages self- control in a child.

Encourage children to take the perspective of others. Talk to children about the effects of their behavior on others. (How would you feel if Keisha did that to you?) This role – playing approach fosters moral development and empathy in children.

Enforce rules consistently. Children need to have a clear idea about what is expected of them and to know that there will be consequences when they fail to meet your standards. This practice also fosters self-control in children." The end of what's taken from the book. Now I will give effective ways to punish them from that same book. First I want to explain the importance of punishing them. When you do so. Your motive should be to correct them and never to destroy them mentally, spiritually, or physically. Punishment is from a principle of revenge. On the other had correction is from a principle of love and concern. This is why God tells the father not to provoke their children to wrath, but bring them up in the nurture and admonition of the Lord (Ephesians 6:4) So when you correct them your motive should be to cause them to be better people in life.

Using Punishment Effectively

"To use punishment effectively, Parents should use it less often. That's because punishment often has unintended, negative side effects (Strassberg et al, 1994; Van Houten, 1983) one of these side effects is that punishment often triggers strong negative emotional responses, including fear, anxiety, anger resentment. These emotional reactions can create a variety of problems, including hostility toward parents. A second side effects is heavy punishment can result in general suppression of behavior. In other words, Children who are strongly and frequently punishes may become with drown and inhibited because they fear that any behavior will be punished. Finally, studies show that harsh physical punishment often leads to an increase in aggressive behavior (Weiss et al.,1992) children who are subjected to a lot of physical punishment tend to become more aggressive than the average youngster

Thus, the truckload of side effects associated with punishment make less than ideal as a disciplinary procedure. Although parents probably overuse punishment as a means of behavioral control, it does have a role to play in disciplinary efforts. The following guide lines summarize research evidence on how to make punishment effective while minimizing its side effects (Berkowitz, 1993)

Punishment should not damage the child's self-esteem

To be effective, punishment should get across the message that is the behavior that is undesirable, not the child, unduly harsh physical punishment, derogatory accusations, and other hurtful word erode the child self-esteem.

Punishment should be swift

A delay in delivering punishment undermines its impact. A parent who says, "Wait until your father (or mother) gets home…." Is making a fundamental mistake. (He or She is also unfairly setting up the other parent as the heavy") quick punishment highlights the connection between the prohibited behavior and its negative outcome.

Punishment should be consistent

If you want to eliminate an undesirable behavior, you should punish it every time it occurs. When parents are inconsistent about punishing a particular behavior, they only create confusion in the child.

Punishment should be explained

When children are punished, the reason for their punishment should be explained as fully as possible, given the reason they are punished, the more effective the punishment tends to be. These explanations, characteristic of the authoritative style, also foster the development of self-control.

Point out alternative, positive ways for your child to behave and reinforce these actions.

One shortcoming of punishment is that it only tells a child what not to do. A better strategy is to punish an undesirable response and reward a positive alternative behavior. Children usually engage in undesirable behavior for a reason. Suggest another response that serves the same purpose and reward a child for doing it. For example many troublesome behaviors exhibited by children are primarily attention seeking devices. Punishment of these responses will be more effective if you can provide a child with more acceptable ways to gain attention." This ends what is taken out of the psychology book. Now let's go to number 8

8. Nourish your household

This means to provide with food or other nutriment necessary for life and growth: feed to foster the development of: Promote to keep alive. This means more than just going to the store and buying food to give them. It also means giving them the right foods with the right nutriment. This will keep them alive yes you can allow or send your wife to do grocery shopping or your maid. You in turn must oversee what's entering your home being the head. When you nourish them mentally also spiritual for life this means everything that involves bringing them up.

9. The blesser

This is a powerful thing because according to God death and life are in the power of your tongue (Proverbs 18:21) Your tongue sets on fire the course of nature (James 3:6) God blessed Adam and eve before he created them by speaking into their lives what he wanted them to be and do (Genesis 1:28) God spoke words over Noah and his family (v.9:1) Isaac blessed his son Jacob with words speaking material and spiritual things (Genesis 27: 22-29) Jacob stretched out his hands and blessed his son (48:13,14) He also blessed his son Joseph saying (v.15,16)

What is the point? The man is the spiritual authority in his home. You have the power to speak blessings into your family tree. For those of you who don't agree, stating "I don't believe in the bible." Well you don't have to. That will be your lost. I'm a living witness of the power of the tongue. This is something you can't get around a change life. I was a little child and one of my family members spoke over me that I will be a heartbreaker. So as a result I grew up making girls cry, breaking their hearts. Another one of my family members (RIP) spoke over me and my little brothers' life –Albert stating that we will be like our uncle Big Albert and Benhur going back and forth to prison. I spent a lot of years in prison. I'm only 30 years old at the time of this writing. My little brother spent time in and out of prison; He is currently in prison serving an 8 year sentence. So if this is effective in the negative way, why can't it be effective in a positive way? So take your children and wife and speak good things in and over their lives. Don't tell them that won't ever be anything because they make mistakes. When they come to you with their plans bless them and build their confidence up.

10. He is morally correct

This is the life of a gentleman. He has to be morally correct so he can teach his household to be mentally, spiritually, and physically as he is. His ways are right toward everyone. He speaks with respect to his elders. Yes sir, no sir. He knows his posture at the dinner table, in the bedroom, outside the house, in the work place, etc. His words are used wisely. He guides his home in the ways of God.

11. He is trusted

He can be trusted by outsiders. To them, he is the best man to be in business with. He is the best man working for. People know that he will treat them right. His wife knows that he will be faithful. She never worries about him sleeping, leading, flirting, touching, or kissing another woman. This is beneath him. He despises this. He honors his body and knows this is what separates the faithful individual from the unfaithful one. His family trusts him to be supportive of them in their goals and plains in life. Whoever comes in contact with him. They learn quickly that he is a man that could be trusted. He is a gentleman.

12. He is a giver

He gives of his time, strength, love, money, trust, ability to all – God, his family and outsiders. He understands that the wife needs time with him and the children. So he makes it happen because he is a gentleman. I believe the gentleman and faithful man is preceded. Then who is the man. This is the man who doesn't do that which is becoming of the gentleman.

PART TWO

Organisms dying off

I believe that to everything in life there is a right and a wrong way to do something. I like to say that there is a right and a wrong environment to function in. Whenever you live in the wrong environment, you will become an organism that's dying off until you are DEAD- Yet you will suffer in the process.

Written by Glenn C. Damond © 2014

Chapter 1

Organisms (people) dying off in their sex.

Organism is defined as any individual animal or plant having diverse organs and parts that function together as a whole to maintain life and its activities. Anything resembling a living thing in its complexity of structure or functions.

I will use organisms to refer to people. We as people commit ourselves to certain habits and lifestyles that cause us to die off slowly but inevitably. This is because people persist in that pet lifestyle without ever wanting to change. They live with concept "we all have to die from something, or die anyway." They say this until they are affected. This is any discomfort, any departure from health, a particular destructive process in an organ or organism, with a specific cause and characteristic symptoms. Any harmful or destructive condition." Hence the title organisms dying off. Once you receive what the lifestyle produces, you begin to live your life in discomfort. The destructive process. If I have sex once with the wrong person, I could receive a STD (Sexually Transmitted Disease.) Then the process begins. You add to the dying process by stressing, worrying, etc. If I begin smoking tobacco, I could catch a stroke, cancer, bladder and kidney cancer's, etc. I will deal with these and much more in detail to show you how organisms dye off all because of the lifestyles they indulge in. They live for the moment and end up being sorry when their own desired lifestyle produces a negative result. I will begin with one the most powerful functions-sex.

Sex

I have to start off by saying that sex is a gift given by God to his creation. It's given to enjoy and reproduce, but only in his divine plan. His plan is marriage. Whenever we step outside of his plan which is waiting until we are married. We begin to die off. It is because of the misuse of this that many relationships are destroyed, children are abused, and families are separated. God can't make a mistake. So when you follow his divine principles in regards to sex. You will live in peace and enjoy it. You won't become an organism that's dying off. Sex for some represents great intimacy and moments of remember able pleasure. Others rather indulge in it trying to fill some kind of void. Women and men at times use it to make each other upset. This is done when a couple has difficulties that arose between them. Then one of them would go and have sex with someone other than their mate, this can lead to a break up, a beaten, a killing etc. The reason is simple. Organism functioning outside of its divine purpose. In the book of Genesis, chapter 1 verse 27, lets read "So God created man in his own image, in the image of God created he him; male and female created he them. "I'll deal with organism dying off in relationships in the next chapter. One of the spiritual truths in this verse is that he created them before he ever separated them in that second chapter of the same book. He created them one because he originally ordained for them to receive everything that's right within that relationship

Now I will give you God's view on sex and psychologist's view. Before I must let you know that whenever you step outside of God's plan for sex you suffer. You become the organism that dies off. God is not trying to keep you from sex. He wants you to enjoy it until you die, but the enjoyment in his plan will be in peace.

Psychologist's View

Before I begin I need to point out that sex research is subject to some unique problems. For one thing, researchers have a particularly difficult time getting representative samples of the subjects. Most studies of American sexuality are over resented with white, middle class volunteers. Also, many individuals are not willing according to (strassberg Lowe, 1995) are more liberal and more sexually experienced. Than the general population. Unfortunately, people may respond less than truthfully about their sex lives because of shame, embarrassment, boasting, or wishful thinking. This and what follows is taken from" psychology Applied to Modern life"

Key aspects of sexual Identity

Identity refers to a clear and stable sense of who is in the larger society. I'll use the term sexual identity to refer to the complex of personal qualities, self- perceptions, attitudes, values, and preferences that guide one's sexual behavior.

In other words, your sexual identity is your sense of yourself as a sexual person. It includes four key features: sexual orientation, body image, sexual values and ethics, and erotic preferences.

Sexual Orientation

Sexual orientation is an individual's preference for emotional and sexual relationship with individuals of one gender or the other. Heterosexuals seek emotional – sexual relationships with members of the other gender. Homosexuals seek emotional- sexual relationships with the same genders. In recent years, the terms gay and straight have become widely used to refer to homosexuals and heterosexuals, respectively. Male homosexuals are called gay, whereas female homosexuals prefer to be called lesbians.

Body Image

Your body image is how you see yourself physically. Your view of your physical self definitely affects how you feel about yourself in sexual domain. A positive body image is correlated with greater sexual activity and higher sexual satisfaction (Hatfield Rapson, 1996) White ultra-thinness for women has been a long- time media message, muscular body types for men are getting more promotion (Daniluk, 1998; Pope, Phillips, olivardia, 2000). The increasing popularity of gym memberships and plastic surgery for facelifts and breast enhancements testifies to the importance of body image.

Sexual values and ethics

All cultures impose constraints on how people are expected to behave sexually. People are taught that certain expressions of sexuality are "right" while others are "wrong". The nature of these sexual messages varies depending on gender, race, ethnicity, and socioeconomic status. For example, the double standard encourages sexual experimentation in males, but not females. Individuals are faced with the daunting task of sorting through these often conflicting messages to develop their own sexual values and ethics.

Erotic Preferences

Within the limits imposed by sexual orientation and values, people still differ in what they find enjoyable. Your erotic preferences encompass your attitudes about self-stimulation, oral sex, intercourse, and other sexual activities. They develop through a complex inter play of physiological and psychosocial influences. Key aspects of sexual Identity is taken from the book "Psychology Applied to Modern life." I will deal with 1and 4. This will be in regards to God's view verses psychologist's view. Everyone has their own way of doing things, but I will show you how organisms die off in their sex lives. I believe everyone can agree with me when I say that a lot of sexual activities we indulge in we don't experience peace. The truth of the matter is, we are deeply yearning for peace, but we involve ourselves in things we think will bring us peace. Instead we remain angry and frustrated. This is not God's desire. He desires you to have peace in what he ordained. This is why we have to do it as he planned. I'll say again. We all can agree that God can't make a mistake.

If he planned for a women and man to be together, when you follow his principles in the matter it will last. When we don't we die off as organisms. God's principles we will say is the environment where we live. When we step outside this environment in regards to sex we begin to die off.

Now back to the first key "Sexual orientation" it's an individual's preference for emotional and sexual relationships with individuals of one gender or the other. Heterosexuals: they seek emotional – sexual relationships with members of the other gender. This is God's plan before sex, the woman and the man. (Genesis 2:24) Therefore shall a man leave his father and his mother, and shall cleave unto his wife: and they shall be one flesh." That one flesh is marriage which is honorable in all men or to be honored by all (Hebrews 13:4). This is when sex becomes pure or unsoiled.

Marital Sex

This is taken from the book "psychology Applied to Modern life" there is ample evidence that a couple overall marital satisfaction is highly related to their satisfaction is highly related to their satisfaction with their sexual relationship (Christopher sprecher, 2000) Thus, good sex and a good marriage tend to go hand and hand. Of course, it is difficult to tell whether this a matter of good sex promoting good marriages or good marriages promoting good sex. In all probability, it's a two Way Street It seems likely that marital closeness is conducive to sexual pleasure and that sexual satisfaction increases marital satisfaction. Married couples vary greatly in how often they have sex. On the average, couples in their 20's and 30 are engage in sex about two or three times a week.

The frequency of sex among married couples tends to decrease as the years wear on.

According to psychologists this is a natural function, but not all sex couples sex life tends to decrease. This is when I believe couples begin to function in uncontrolled sex lives. At this point individuals no longer are satisfactory for you. This is why God wants us to maintain self-control in every area of our life. (Galatians 5: 22-23).

Self-Control in Sex

Self- control is the environment God desires. When we step outside this environment we begin to die off. I will show you the following is taken from "Psychology Applied to Modern life."

Infidelity in committed Relationships

Sexual infidelity occurs when a person who is in a committed relationship engages in erotic activity with someone other than his or her partner. Among married couples this behavior is also called "adultery "or "extra marital sex". The vast majority of people (90%) in our society believe that extramarital sex is "always "or "almost always wrong "(Treas & Giesen, 2000). Although it's not common, extramarital sex can be consensual.

Two examples include "swinging "and open marriage. "Swinging typically involves married couples exchanging partners for sex or both partners having sex with a third person.

In "open marriage" both partners agree that it is okay for each to have sex with others (O'Neil & O'Neill 1972) as we noted, gay male's couples are more likely to have "open marriages" Then there are lesbian or married couples. Precisely what kind of erotic activity qualifies as "cheating "is debatable especially between men and women? The question is asked are you unfaithful if you develop a deep emotional involvement without sex? No doubt many people would say "Yes" one researcher found that emotional affairs (Thompson, 1984). Such affairs often occur over the telephone or the Internet . The Internet has added confusion to an already complex issue. For example is it "Cheating "if a person in a committed relationship uses the Internet for sexual arousal or masturbation? What about exchanging sexually explicit e-mail with another person you never meet face to face? Therapists are beginning to see more couples with Internet-related concerns (Schnarch, 1997).

Now Infidelity occurs when organisms function outside self-control. This is when we get in the lust realm. That book of Matthew 5:28 state that whosoever looketh on a woman to lust after is guilty of committing adultery. The Greek text of the bible translates lust as one to set the heart upon that is long for. When organisms enter this area this is when swinging comes into the picture. The process of dying starts because God's plan is that every man have his own wife, and let every woman has her own husband (1 Corinthians 7:2) His plan is one man and one woman and not open marriages.

Dying Off

When we engage in sexual relations with someone outside the marriage we then become one with that person (1 Corinthians 6:16, 17) Sex is something spiritual. So when you connect sexually, your spirits are connecting. This is why you will always have feelings for that person. You say you love them to death when they are cheating on you. The relationship begins to die off. Your emotions, love, will, sex life, etc. becomes divided. This will present problems for you and your mate. Why would or did this happen? It's because individuals are functioning outside of the proper environment for sex. When we function outside the environment we get into swinging, open marriages, homosexuality, phone or Internet sex, etc. The process of dying begins.

A homosexual seeks emotional-sexual relationships with members of the same gender. The process of dying off my mother was a lesbian for years. Right now she goes straight and having participated in lesbian activity. How did she or is she dying off? As I write this march the 15, 2008, my mother has AIDS stemming from a life she started when I was under ten years old. The process of dying had been beginning on her. She also suffers from sugar diabetes. She isn't trying to do anything to help herself. As a matter of fact, she is sprung out on crack cocaine.
Let's take a look at the psychologists view on the origin of Homosexuals. The following is taken from the book "Psychology Applied to Modern life"

Origins

Why do some people become straight and others gay? I will focus on possible causes of homosexuality because relatively little has been written about the causes of heterosexuality (a reflection of heterosexism). A number of environmental explanations have been suggested as causes of homosexuality. Freud believed that homosexuality originated from an unresolved Oedipus complex. That is instead of coming to identify with the parent of the same gender, the child continues to identify with the parent of the same gender, and the child continues to identify with the parent of the gender. Sociologists propose that homosexuality develops because of poor relationships with same- gender peers or because being labeled a homosexual sets up a self-fulfilling prophecy. Learning theorists assert that homosexuality results from early positive homosexual experiences. Surprisingly, the most comprehensive study of the causes of sexual orientation found no compelling support for any of these leading environmental explanations of homosexuality (Bell, Weinberg,& Hammersmith,1981) On a related issue, no evidence has been found that parents sexual orientation is linked to that of their children (That is, heterosexual parents are as likely to produce homosexual parents are as likely to produce homosexual (or heterosexual offspring as homosexual parents are children who grow up in gay or lesbian families are predominantly heterosexual (Patterson, 1992).

The Bible's View

Researches after research have been conducted. Now let's go to the real origin and where it starts from. First I want to say that God created us, as you all should know. If we were created by him he has the best plan for all of us. But ask yourself the question. How will you know the plan of God if you reject God? How will you know his plan if you don't want have nothing to do with him?

Do you think that he will reveal his plan to you if you have no relationship with him? I don't believe so. In the book of Romans chapter 1 verse 18 we find that God's wrath or judgment is revealed(the Greek text reads revealed to mean to take off the cover, that is disclosed)from heaven against all ungodliness(this is those who have no reverence for God or scared things).

I will deal with the homosexual right now. Romans 1:26-27 records "For this cause (the cause of apostasy, not wanting anything to do with God) God gave them up to vile affections: for even their women did change the natural use (this is lesbianism) into that which is against nature:

And likewise also the men, leaving the natural use of the woman, burned (were inflamed)in their lust one toward another; men with men working that which is unseemly, and receiving in themselves that recompense of their error which was meet."

Now anyone with common sense would know that this is lesbianism and homosexuality. Now let's break it down a little to convey a better understanding.

The bible says that women did change the natural use into that which is against nature. I am talking about organisms dying off.

The Greek text reads physical for natural and natural production for nature. So in essence we could read it like this, "For even their women did change the physical use into that which is against natural production. We come up with a better understanding of this. Men also leaving the physical use of the woman and burn in their lust (excitement of the mind, that is longing after) one toward another.

It's not natural for a man to desire a man or a woman to desire a woman. I already revealed to you God's plan for the man and woman. When this plan is perverted and becomes unnatural. You as an organism begin to die off. You are never satisfied because you stepped out of the environment of self-control. You can't reproduce because you stepped out of the natural environment for reproduction.

The following is taken from the college book "Psychology Applied to Modern life." The best advice I could give you is to incorporate the following within your intimate relationship. Be the individual who refuse to view their mate as a sex object, but as a friend.

It's hard to overestimate the importance of friends. They provide help in times of need, advice in times of confusion, consolation in times of failure, and praise in times of achievement.

The importance of friends was underscored in a survey of 40,000 readers of Psychology in a crisis they were more likely to turn to friends than to family for help."

Now let's take a close look at the above paragraph. Friends provide help in times of need, advice in times of confusion, consolation in times of failure, and praise in times of achievement.

(Before I go on let me say this, there is nothing wrong with having friends. But let your mate be your first friend as she is your first lady or first man. Nor am I'm implicating that you are wrong when you turn to a friend for help, advice in times of confusion etc.

My point is that your mate should be that first friend as I said before. God ordained everything to be received within that relationship. This is why it is important for the man and the woman to equip them mentally, spiritually and physically to be able to meet their mates need.)

Help in Times of Need

A friend can help you in many ways. It could be to pay a bill, car note because you are unable to do so. There is nothing wrong with this. But the mate, I will go as far as to say that is out of order if they can't help pay bills with their mate. Something is wrong with that picture.

I know females right now today that have boyfriends and they constantly step outside their relationship to get more money or attention. They have no morals and dignity for themselves.

I could look at their lifestyles and see that they are in an incomplete relationship. When they step outside to someone they consider a friend, it leads to other things.

If it's the female, which I see on a regular basis, sex comes afterward. The male sees in his mind how sexy she is. The female knows that he likes her and not only looks at her as a friend. So she uses this to her advantage. She may move a certain way seductively when she sees him looking at her with passion in his eyes.

When she knows she has his attention, she feels she could get him to do anything she asks. She only has to make him think he will have sex with her.

Sex could come afterward in exchange for money. Now her self-respect is gone. When she's around that person she acts a certain way because she doesn't want him to expose her to a man she may really like and don't want him to know what she did in life or the man she's with that she plans to marry.

Why did this happen? What happened? What happen was the female begins to die off while she is in a relationship with one man. She allowed another man to take her self-respect.

He could come around her and play with her in a sexual way. She may or may not like it or she may allow him or stop him. Then out of anger he exposes her in front of her boyfriend which could lead to a fight or killing .Why did this happen? It happened because this female stepped outside of her relationship with her man to receive financial support by degrading herself.

herself. This may affect relationships in the future. It can destroy the intimate one she is in. This is organisms dying off in their intimate relationships

Advice in Times of Confusion

I met a female a few days ago that I really came to like. I talked about her in another chapter. When you read that chapter you will know why.

So this female I came to be very attracted to. Her ways are very whorish. I knew she was in a superficial relationship. I believe that certain women wouldn't behave in that manner if they had a complete man or the right man. This is why I approached her on that level. She gave me the attention. During this time we got on different levels becoming closer to the point where we would just stare at each other.

One day she was talking to someone and she spoke with anger in her voice. I called her to see what was wrong with her. She broke down and expressed herself to me as if she was about to cry. Prior to this never opened up to me. The day before this I just had got on her for not opening up to me. My point is, she should have told me that she was stressing. One of the things she was stressing behind was school. She told me that she was behind in her school work and that couldn't go or expect her boyfriend to help her.

So, me being her friend at the time and also trying to be her man, I started a college course similar to the one she was taking to be able to relate to her. She told me she had a tutor before I started to study law.

She still stayed behind in school. She didn't even know I started this course until we got on bad terms. I just use to give her law questions to answer. I always asked her what she did in school that day and we would talk about it.

I was able to give her advice in times of confusion. This was why I was a friend trying to be her man. I was able to communicate with her concerning things only she and her boyfriend is supposed to talk about. She opened herself up for me to do things that supposed to be off limits for friends. Her boyfriend wasn't able to give her advice so she received it from other men. No telling what she allowed other men beside me do. This was done while we (I) was her friend.

In that situation, I would have familiarized myself to be able to be my mate's friend in that situation. Maybe you can't afford a college course. Then I would take the time out to study with her.

In this situation, I'm also revealing to you the difference between a woman and a lady. For now, a woman who doesn't have the attributes of a lady may do things that would cause her relationship to fail. She caused it. The lady on the other hand had morals but won't break them at the expense of her self-respect. She understands that there are other means by which she could maintain her self-dignity.

Consolation in Times of Failure

I believe females and males are good at this. I mean they naturally pick, or encourage their mate when things aren't going right or they have failed in one of their endeavors in life.

Praise in Times of Achievement

I also believe females and males are good in praising in times of achievement. Of course I'm not saying that every male and female are like this but I believe majority are. Couples find it exultant to praise each other for job promotions, good business deals, etc.

The following is taking from the college book, "Psychology Applied to Modern Life." So, incorporate the following in your intimate relationships.

What Makes a Good Friend

"The most intriguing aspect of this survey was its investigation of what makes a "good friend." Loyalty is the heart and soul of friendship. There is confidences (an aspect of loyalty). Then there is warmth/affection and supportiveness, a sense of humor. Then there is a willingness to let friends be themselves (Block, 1980). Block points out that people often put others under pressure to behave in ways that are consistent with their own expectation such "conditional" expectations would appear to resemble those held by many parents for their children.

Psychologist Carl Rogers believed that conditional affection contributed to distortions in people's self-concepts. He therefore advocated unconditional acceptance in child-rearing. Consistent with Roger's theory, Block's respondents emphasized the importance of unconditional acceptance from their friends.

A slightly different way of looking at what is important in friendship comes from a cross-cultural study of students in England, Italy, Japan, and Hong Kong (Argyle & Henderson, 1984). The investigators wanted to see whether they could find enough agreement on how friends should conduct themselves to permit the formulation of some informal rules governing friendships on the basis of the student's response, the authors were able to identify six informal rules.

The Rules of Friendship

- Share news of success with a friend
- Show emotional support
- Volunteer help in time of need
- Strive to make a friend happy when in each other's company
- Trust and confide in each other
- Stand up for a friend in his or her absence"

Now let's go back up to what makes a good friend and break some of these qualities down. Particularly I want to deal with loyalty, warmth/affection, supportiveness, and a sense of humor.

Loyalty

Incorporating loyalty within your intimate relationship is vital. You show loyalty in the friendship area with another woman or man. You won't allow the friendship to go beyond limits of friendship.

Because when you are loyal, you are faithful to that person. To step outside of loyalty is to be unfaithful and results in organisms dying off in their intimate relationships.

To be faithful means I won't allow another man to touch me sexually even if he supplies the attention or financial support that my man can't supply or isn't supplying. To be unfaithful means that I will suffer and work with my man to try to help him understand that I need his attention, etc.

Warmth/Affection

These two go hand and hand. God put forth a divine principle in regards to affection. When you stay inside of this environment you will be productive and live. When you step outside this environment you will begin to die off in your intimate relationship.

Outside this Environment

I will just say this because I deal with this in a later chapter entitled. "The best relationship to be in." I revealed how stepping outside of this environment causes trouble between you and your mate.

Because of what or who you give your affection to be whom or what you will desire. This is why the principle I'm about to show you is so powerful and vital for you to maintain within your intimate relationship.

Inside this Enviroment

In the book of Proverbs this divine principle is recorded.

Let thy fountain be blessed and rejoice with the wife of thy youth.

Let her breasts satisfy thee at all times; and thou ravished always with her love

(v 18, 19)."

The Powerful Principle affection

This divine principle is so powerful and it holds true. I really until this day 3-29-08 desired to fall in love with a beautiful woman in spirit and beautifully in appearance. I met two different women on two different occasions.

The truth was that I approached both of these women and seriously; desired to fall in love with. I asked both of them to have my son.

My point is I really got attached to these females while they had boyfriends and one of them told me that they were in a relationship but it wasn't serious. The other one told me that she was in a relationship with the same guy for 9 years. They allowed me to do things I was not supposed to do and talk about things that only is should to be discussed between them and their mate.

This leads me to believe that they were both in incomplete relationships. I also believe I was too strong mentally for them.

In time of giving all of my attention and affection to them, I really got to the point where I had to see them and had to talk to them to hear their voice. I had to be around them. I always kept them on my mind. I wasn't in love. My objective was to fall in love with them.

The power of affection was in operation until the point another woman didn't even matter to me. I gave all of my affection to them because I was really sincere and serious about them. This is something usual for me considering my past and me thinking I would never fall in love.

I believe now I made two mistakes in deciding to dedicate my heart to them. I'm willing to fall in love and I was rushing into a relationship with them.

And because of the powerful principle affection was operating, even though it was exercise in error-meaning with females already in relationships. It was hard for me to just walk away from them. Both of them are beautiful, the same height and very feisty, and going to college. They were young about five or six years younger than me but in their twenties. They both been hurt before by men, had no morals and this is why they gave sexual favors for money. They could easily be penetrated because the situation (relationship) wasn't right. I really don't know the details behind that. When I talked to them I don't talk about another man.

The point I'm trying to convey is the power of affection was in operation; was at work. I tried to rush days through just so I could see and talk to them. When I couldn't see them it would affect my writing. I mean I love to write, but this how powerful this principle is.

Now bring it within the intimate relationship as being exercised as friendship. This would be the intimate/friendship relationship.

The verse says let her breasts satisfy you at all and be thou ravished always with her love

The words all times and always are used to convey this divine principle. This means at all times and always let her breasts satisfy you. This means also if you start desiring another woman's breasts you have stepped outside of the divine principle. This will lead to trouble.

Breasts also mean the seat of love. This is taken from the Hebrew meaning. When you sit somewhere you remain in that position until you move. I know when you move out of that seat, your position changes, as in the intimate relationship/friendship. When you seat in the breasts of your wife as your seat of love, you are within the proper environment. When you change positions desiring another woman's breast, the relationship will begin to die off because you are about to start performing the divine principle of affection on another woman.

You will see another woman breasts. The bible tells us to let your wife's breasts satisfy you at all times. So that other woman's breast shouldn't even matter to you. Because you are satisfied with the ones you have at home.

The verse also says to be thou ravished always with her love. To do this means to be bathed, satiated, and soaked with her love. When you get to this point another woman wouldn't even matter you. The ideal of ravish also means to be intoxicated with her love. This means to be excited beyond self-control. This isn't a self-control that steps outside of the divine principle of self-control this one that's filled with overwhelming joy or happiness at the thought of your girl. Because when you experience intoxication of her love, you have a feeling of wild excitement in a good manner.

<u>A Support System</u>

It's vital to provide support to your friends. Now incorporate this within your intimate relationship/friendship. Then you will become organisms that are living because they function within the proper environment that's suitable for them to live in and not die.

It's important to support your mate in their endeavors in life. There is nothing too wrong with an outside friend to support them but you want this attribute to be in your own mate. This way you won't be vulnerable in that area and another man or woman wouldn't become a threat to your relationship. Since they are being satisfied at home, they are receiving what's right for them in the divine authority.

Remember the principle in the verse in the beginning of this chapter.

A Sense of Humor

I'm just a natural clown. It would be times when I just would react or act a certain way that makes people laugh.

Some individuals are consumed with work, etc. Things can suck the life out of them to point where they rarely smile or laugh. Life is too short and serious for them to take time out to smile and laugh.

Women love men that make them laugh on a constant basis. This could be what attracted them to that individual, her friend. She may be upset and want to go around her and make her laugh.

I believe this will help to keep her mind off the problem. She shouldn't have to go through this at all. She should be able to go home and receive this from her boyfriend.

Proverbs 17:22 records "a merry heart doeth good like a medicine: but a broken spirit drieth the bones."

When we take medicine we do so to get healed from a particular dysfunction. When we stress, etc., laughter is the medicine that keeps you well from the disease of stress. When we stress we become organisms that's dying off.

CHAPTER 2

Organisms Dying Off in Their Intimate Relationships (Part 2)

Let's take it from where I stopped in regards to sense of humor. Individuals become so consumed with work that they neglect their family interactions. There is nothing wrong with working, but there is something wrong with allowing it to interfere with your relationship with your family.

God used the analogy of the ant in the book of Proverbs 6:6-8, to reveal to mankind a lot of different things. In it all, they are balanced because they work together. Not one is neglected or left out. We need to apply this principle to our intimate relationship/friendship.

When we do this work of business endeavors wouldn't get in the way of our family interactions because we would be balanced. I believe the wife will begin to pick arguments, telling you that you are neglecting them. "You don't show up to your son first game, your daughter's first photos shoot and your wife's appointment." The two of you all constantly fight over and over becoming organisms that's dying off in their intimate relationship.

What was the reason? It is simple. She only wants to spend time with your family. The following is taken from the college book "Psychology Applied to Modern Life."

Work and Career Issues

"The possible interactions between one's occupation and one's marriage are numerous and complex. Individuals' job satisfaction and involvement can affect their own marital satisfaction, their partner's marital satisfaction and their children's development.

Work and Marital Adjustment

A host of studies have investigated the relationship between spouses' job satisfaction and their marital adjustment. We could speculate that these two variables might be either positively or negatively related. On the one hand, if a spouse is highly committed to a satisfying career, he or she may have less time and energy to devote to marriage and family.

On the other hand, the frustration and stress of an unsatisfying job might spill over to contaminate one's marriage. The research on this question suggests that both scenarios are realistic possibilities. Both husbands and wives struggle to balance the demands of work and family and both report that work commitments often interfere with family responsibilities (Hochschild, 1997); Milkie & Pettola, 1999). When pressures increase at work, husbands and wives report more role conflicts and often feel overwhelmed by their multiple commitments (Crouter. et al., 1999) Now we must remember that Psychology is the science that studies behavior and the Physiological and mental processes that underlie it, and it is the profession that applies the accumulated knowledge of this science to practical problems.

Behavior is any overt (observable) response or activity by an organism."

So we could conclude that psychologist's research and study individual's behavior patterns. Because this is what they do, I say that to say the following. Those researches are based on people doing and not doing a certain thing. If 50% of people in college gossip you don't have to be a part of this percentage. You could choose to be a part of the percentage that doesn't gossip.

My point is this you can work, pursue a career and still participate in family interactions. You don't have to be of the percentage that becomes the statistics that's failing in that area. They have become organisms dying off in their intimate relationship/friendship. The following is taken from the college book, "Psychology of Applied to Modern Life."

Gender Difference in Friendship

"Men and women same-gender friendships have a lot in common, but there are some interesting differences that appear rooted in traditional gender roles and socialization.

In the United States, women's friendships are more often emotionally based, whereas men tend to be activity based. Although some researchers have challenged this characterization (Walker, 1994), the current belief is that men friendship are typically based on shared interests and doing things together, while women friendships more often focus on talking- usually about feelings and relationships. (Fehr, 1996, 2000).

Obviously, female friends do engage in joint activities, but they often use these occasions to talk and male friends talk, but their conversation are usually focused on activities and non-personal matters-------sports, work, vehicles, and computers (Fehr, 1996, 2000). A related finding is that women are likely to confront friends about conflicts to resolve them, whereas men seem willing to tolerate and work around sources of tension in friendship (wright, 1982).

We can also compare American men and women friendship on preferred topics of conversation. Women are far more likely than men to discuss personal problems, feelings, and people (Caldwell & Peplau, 1982; Davisdson & Duberman, 1982). Men are much more likely to talk about sports, work, and vehicles than personal concerns. Interestingly, men who don't adhere to traditional gender roles seem to divulge as much to their best male friend as most women do to their best female friend (Lavine & Lombardo, 1984)"

I pray you have a complete understanding of how individuals die off in their intimate relationships and upon having that. I pray you now incorporate friendship within your intimate relationships.

CHAPTER 4

Organisms Dying Off When They Indulge in Desired Habits

God tells us to obey our parents that we may live long on the earth (Ephesians 6:1-3). Then it settles the debate. "That one can die before his time."

In today's world, we mourn our loved ones because we were led to believe that they die because it was their time or God took them home. We say this after we knew that they lived a life in rebellion to God.

Explain to me how it is time for a fourteen year old female who haven't finish school. What have she accomplished? Better yet, I will take you to the streets concerning this matter. Take a thirteen year old male, me, who started selling drugs and acting out in school. I almost was killed several times. I explain my life in the book I wrote about my life.

My point is this. What if I would have died? Then would you say that it is was my time? Maybe you would. I watched several of my friends die before seeing seventeen years of age. Was it their time? No.

The truth of the matter is when organisms function outside of their proper environment they die off. I hope you didn't forget how this part started off. Organisms don't just die off in sex and relationships. They also die off when they smoke, drink, etc. Now let's get off into it. The following is taken from the college book "Psychology Applied to Modern life."

Smoking

"The smoking of tobacco is widespread in our culture, with current consumption running around 2400 cigarettes a year per adult in the United States. The percentage of people who smoke has declined noticeably since the mid-1960s. "The prevalence of smoking in the United States, adults who smoke has declined steadily since the mid-1960s. Although considerable progress had been made, smoking still accounts for about 400,000 premature deaths each year. (Data from: Centers for Disease Control).

Nonetheless, about 26% of adult men and 22% of adult women in the United States continue to smoke regularly. Unfortunately, these figures are slightly higher (28% for both sexes) among college students (Rigotti, Lee, & Wechsler, 2000).

Health Effects

Suspicions about the health risks associated with tobacco use were voiced in some quarters early in the 20th Century. However, the risks of smoking were not widely appreciated until the mid-1960s. Since then, accumulating evidence has clearly shown that smokers face a much greater risk of premature death than nonsmokers (Schmitz, Jarvik, & Schneider, 1997). For example, a twenty five year old male who smokes two packs a day has an estimated life expectancy 8.3 years shorter than that of a similar nonsmoker (Schlaadt & Shannon, 1994) The overall risk is positively correlated with the number of cigarettes smoked and their tar and nicotine content. Cigar smoking, which has increased dramatically in recent years, elevates health risks almost as much as cigarette smoking (baker et al, 2000)

Why are mortality rates higher for smokers? Smoking increases the likelihood of developing a surprisingly large range of diseases (Thun, Apicella, & Henley, 2000).

Organisms Dying Off

Health risks associated with smoking, including the three leading causes of death in the modern world-heart attack, cancer, and stroke. Yes smoking can lead to strokes, cancer of larynx, lung cancer, heart attacks (smoking more than doubles risks). Peptic (stomach) ulcers (smokers more vulnerable), Pancreatic cancer (30% linked to smoking) Reproductive system (In women: cervical cancer – In men Impotence), cataracts, mouth (oral) cancer, Esophageal cancer, chronic obstructive lung diseases, Bladder and Kidney cancers, unborn babies at risk for premature birth, low birth weight, stunted development, and infant death if mother smokes.

Health Effects

Lung cancer and heart disease kill the largest number of smokers. However, smokers also have on elevated risk for oral, bladder, and kidney cancer, as well as cancers of the larynx,

esophagus, and pancreas; for arteriosclerosis, hypertension, stroke, and other cardiovascular disease; and for bronchitis, emphysema, and other pulmonary diseases. Most smokers know about the risks associated with tobacco use, but they tend to underestimate the actual risks as applied to themselves (Ayanian & Cleary, 1999).

The dangers of smoking are not limited to smokers themselves. Family members and co-workers who spend a lot of time around smokers are exposed to second-hand smoke or environment tobacco smoke, which can increase their risk for a variety of illnesses, including lung cancer (Wells, 1998), heart disease (Howard et al., 1998), and breast cancer in women (Lash & Aschengrau, 1999). Young children with asthma are particularly vulnerable to the effects of second-hand smoke (Stoddard & miller, 1995)".

Now let's go back to what I said about the proper environment. Second-hand smoke isn't the proper environment for an organism to live in. When I say live I mean live and continue to live in. So when we function in this improper environment we begin to die off. We in time can receive lung cancer, heart diseases, women breast cancer.

But if we give up smoking our health risks decline reasonably quickly (Samet, 1992).

The following is taken from the book "Psychology Applied to Modern Life."

Drinking

"Alcohol rivals tobacco as one of the leading causes of health problems in American society. Alcohol encompasses a variety of beverages containing ethyl alcohol, such as beers up to 40% in 80-proof liquor (or more in higher-proof liquors). Survey data indicate that about half of adults in the United States drink.

Drinking is particularly prevalent on college campuses, according to a large-scale survey by researchers at the Harvard School of Public Health (Wechsler et al., 1994). This survey of over 17,000 undergraduates at 140 schools found that 85% of the students drank. Moreover, 50% of the men and 39% of the women reported that they engage in binge drinking with the intention

of getting drunk. Perhaps most telling, college student spend far more money on alcohol (5.5 billion annually) then they do on their books.

Why Do People Drink?

The effects of alcohol are influenced by the user's experience, motivation, and mood, as well as by the presence of food in the stomach, the proof of the beverage, and the rate of drinking. Thus, there is great variability in how alcohol affects different people on different occasions. Nonetheless, the central effect is a "who cares?" brand of euphoria that temporarily boosts self-esteem as one's problem melt away.

Negative emotions such as tension, worry, anxiety, and depression are dulled, and inhibitions may be loosened. Thus, when first-year college students are asked why they drink, they say it's to relax, to feel less tense in social situations, to keep friends company, and to forget their problems. Of course, many other factors are also at work (Wood, Vinson, & Sher, 2001).

Families and peer-groups often encourage alcohol use. Drinking is a widely endorsed and encouraged social ritual in our culture. Its central role is readily apparent if you think about all the alcohol consumed at weddings, sport events, holidays, parties, and so forth. Moreover, the alcohol industry spends hundreds of millions of dollars on advertising to convince us that drinking is cool, sexy, sophisticated, and harmless.

Organisms Dying Off

Alcohol has side effects which some could be very problematic. Hangovers include headaches, dizziness, nausea, and vomiting.

Alcohol contributes to 30% of all automobile fatalities in the U.S. (Yi et al., 1999). Drunk driving is a major social problem that costs about 12,000 lives every year and is the leading cause of death in young adults.

Alcohol has also been implicated in about half of all home accidents and fire fatalities, and about 70% of drowning (Kinney & Leaton, 1987).

With their inhibitions released, some drinkers become argumentative and prone to aggressions. In the Harvard survey of over 17,000 undergraduates, 34% of the students from "heavy drinking" schools reported that they had been insulted or humiliated by a drunken students, 20% had experienced serious arguments, and 13% had been pushed or assaulted (Wechsler et al., 1994). Worst yet, alcohol appear to contribute to about 90% of student rapes and 95% of violent crime on campus. In society at large, alcohol is associated with a host of violent crimes, including murder, assault, rape, child abuse, and spouse abuse (Maisto, galizio, & Connors, 1995).

Finally, alcohol can also contribute to reckless sexual behavior, which may have ramifications for one's health. In the Harvard survey, 41% of the binge drinkers reported that they had unplanned sex as a result of drinking, and 22% indicated that their drinking had led to unprotected sex. I spoke of this early

Heavy drinking increases the risk for heart disease, hypertension; and stroke. Excessive drinking is also correlated with an elevated risk for various types of cancer, including oral, stomach, pancreatic, colon, and rectal cancer.

Serious drinking problems can lead to cirrhosis of the liver, malnutrition, pregnancy complications, brain damage, and neurological disorders.

Finally, alcoholism can produce severe psychotic states, characterized by delirium, disorientation, and hallucinations."

Now let's say a person dies in a car wreck or gets brain damage, etc. Would you say we all have or had to die? Or would you say we all have or had to die from something? I like this one. If you receive brain damage, would you say God allowed this to happen to you? The truth of the matter is as I continue to say over and over again. When organisms function outside of their proper environment they die off.

Drinking destroys lives. So why would this be a proper environment for anyone to live. You not only affect you. You can affect an unborn child.

I'm talking about organisms dying off. You could kill your child before conception while you are also in a dying process.

Still if the child is born, children of alcoholics grow up in dysfunctional environments in which the risk of physical or sexual abuse is much higher than normal (Mathew et al., 1993). The following also is taken from "Psychology Applied to Modern Life."

The Process of Dying Off

The National Institute on alcohol abuse and alcoholism estimates that alcohol costs the U.S. economy about 166 billion annually.

Now let's take a look closely at the process of organisms dying off.

Brain and Central Nervous System

This process of death damages and eventually destroys brain cells, impairs memory, dulls senses, impairs physical coordination, affect judgment, reasoning, and inhibitions.

Immune System

This process of dying lowers resistance to disease. If your immune system can't fight for you, then something can overcome and destroy you.

Liver

Alcohol damages and eventually destroys liver cells, causes medical conditions including fatty liver, alcohol hepatitis, and cirrhosis.

Gastrointestinal Tract

Alcohol causes inflammation, may cause cancer, and leads to pancreatitis

Heart

It may raise blood pressure, cause irregular heartbeat, and cause heart disease and stroke.

Stomach and Intestines

May cause bleeding and inflammation and may trigger cancer.

Reproductive System

In women, menstrual cycles become irregular; pregnant women have an increased risk of bearing children with birth defects. In men, hormone levels may be altered; impotence may occur; testicles may atrophy.

Now let's get into another dangerous area. Taken from the book "Psychology Applied to Modern Life."

Overeating

Obesity is a common health problem. The criteria for obesity vary considerably. One simple, intermediate criterion is to classify people as obese of their weight exceeds their ideal body weight by 20%. If this criterion is used, 31% of men and 35% of women in the United States qualify as obese (Brownell & Wadden, 2000). Many experts prefer to assess obesity in terms of body mass survey show surprisingly sharp increases in the incidence of obesity (Jeffery, 2001, Mokdad et al., 1999). If a BMI over 25 is used as the cutoff, over 50% of American adults are struggling with weight problems!

Obesity is similar to smoking in that it exerts a relatively subtle impact on health that is easy for many people to ignore. Nevertheless, the long-range effects of obesity are a significant health problem that elevates one's mortality risk (Bender et al., 1999, Allison et al., 1999). Overweight people are more vulnerable than others to heart disease, diabetes, hypertension, respiratory problems, gall bladder disease, stroke, arthritis, muscle and joint pain, and back problems (Must et al., 1999, Pi-Sunyer, 1995).

Excessive eating and inadequate exercise

The bottom line for overweight people is that their energy intake from food consumption chronically exceeds their energy expenditure from physical activities and resting metabolic processes. In other words, they eat too much in relation to their level of exercise. Ironically, for many years studies in which people maintained food diaries suggested that obese people did not eat much more than people of normal weight (Rodin et al., 1989). However, improved methods of estimating subject's caloric intake and that they typically do eat more than people who are not overweight (Wing & Polley, 2001).

In modern America, the tendency to overeat is easy to understand. Tasty, caloric, high-fat foods are readily available nearly everywhere, not just in restaurants and grocery stores but places.

Unfortunately, the increased availability of highly caloric food in American has been paralleled by declining physical activity (Hill & Peters, 1998). Modern conveniences, such as cars and elevators, and changes in the world of work, such as the shift to more desk jobs, have conspired to make American lifestyles more sedentary than ever before.

Poor Nutrition

Nutrition is a collection of processes (Mainly food consumption) through which an organism utilizes the materials (nutrient) required for survival and growth.

The term also refers to the study of these processes. Unfortunately, most of don't study nutrition very much. Moreover, the cunning mass marketing of nutritionally worthless foods makes it more and more difficult to maintain sound nutritional habits.

Nutrition and Health

Evidence is accumulating that pattern of nutrition influence susceptibility to a variety of diseases and health problems. For example, in a study of over 42,000 women, investigators

Found an association between a measure of overall diet quality and mortality. Women who reported poorer quality diets had elevated mortality rates (Kant et al., 2000).

What are the specific links between diet and health? In addition to the problems associated with obesity, which we have already discussed, other possible connections between eating patterns and health include the following:

1. Heavy consumption of foods that elevate serum cholesterol level (eggs, cheese, butter, shellfish, sausage, and the like) appears to increase the risk of cardiovascular disease (Stamler et al., 2000). Eating habits are only one of several factors that influence serum cholesterol level, but they do make an important contribution. Vulnerability to cardiovascular diseases may also be influenced by other dietary factors. For example, low fiber diets may increase the likelihood of coronary disease (Ludwig et al., 1999; Wolk et al., 1999).
2. High salt intake is thought to be a contributing factor in the development of hypertension (Messerli, Schmieder, & Weir, 1997), although there is still some debate about its exact role.
3. High caffeine consumption may elevate one's risk for hypertension (Lovallo et al., 1996) and for coronary disease (Grossarth-Maticek & Eysenck, 1991). However, the evidence is mixed, and a large-scale study found no association between caffeine consumption and cardiovascular risk (Grobbee et al., 1990). Given these inconsistent findings, more research is needed to settle the issue.
4. High fat diets have been implicated as possible contributors to some forms of cancer, especially prostate cancer (Rose, 1997), and breast cancer (Wynder et al., 1997). Some studies also suggest that high-fiber diets may reduce one's risk for colon and rectal cancer (Reddy, 1999), but the evidence is not conclusive.
5. Vulnerability to osteoporosis, an abnormal loss of bone mass observed most commonly in postmenopausal women, appears to be elevated by a lifelong pattern of inadequate calcium intake (Fahey & Gallagherallred, 1990).
6. Although the research findings are mixed, there are some evidence that high intake of vitamin E may reduce one's risk for coronary disease (Lonn & Yusuf, 1997)

7. Nutritional patterns play a role in the course and management of a host of disease. Prominent examples include gallstones, kidney stones, gout, peptic ulcers, and rheumatoid arthritis (Werbach, 1988). Eating habits may also contribute to the causation of some of these diseases, although the evidence is less compelling on this point.

   Of course, nutritional habits interact with other factors- genetics, exercise, and so on-to determine whether someone will develop a particular disease. Nonetheless, the examples just described indicated that eating habits can influence physical health.

PART THREE

The Best Relationship to be in

Relationships don't fail. People fail by not having an understanding of the right principle to live by. Relationships are unseen entities perpetrated by the parties involved. They aren't designed to stress you or be up and down, but rather to assist you to propel forward in life.

People say we all have our problems. That's true, but I'm talking about matters of the heart. She doesn't have to cry. I don't have to walk in the room and find my girl having sex with another man. Solomon had 1000 women. He can teach you about the immoral woman and the lady- the only two kinds of women you will be dealing with.

So why do I have to go through all of that pain falling in love with an immoral woman when Solomon warned me about her 1000s of years ago.

© 2014 by Glenn C. Damond

CHAPTER 1

Half relationships (In the Work Place)

Now this is a killer of every relationship. It doesn't matter who you are in a relationship with. If you are halfhearted, the relationship won't last long.

When I say half relationship I mean that you're in a relationship and not totally committed to it.

Now you must understand that this commitment varies based on the agreement between the two parties involved.

Let's say you work with someone in a certain job. You don't have to be totally committed. I know you are trying to figure out how you can be totally committed and not be totally committed.

I will show you. It's based on the person and the relationship you have with them. You will never have the same relationship with your business man partner as you have with your wife.

Now speaking about a committed man to his wife and at the same time has a man as business partner. The two of you have what is called a work relationship and it should stay at work. This relationship only extends to working together to get the job done and making the business more successful.

Now this is not to say a couple can't work together or friends can't be more than business partners. This is just to show you an example of what I'm trying to convey.

Once you and your work partner, after getting an understanding, knows that the relationship is and stays at work.

When you come to your wife or your girl, the relationship extends all the way without limitations. You can kiss your wife. You can't kiss your work or business partner.

Both require dedication, trust, commitment, sacrifice, submission, communication, and respect, but it's different when you talk about an intimate relationship between a woman and a man. I will talk about them both.

First, let's deal with the work place and you'll see from each requirement that it is necessary to succeed in life. Then I will deal with the relationship between the woman and the man. So let's begin.

1. Dedication

To dedicate means to set apart for a special use. To commit to oneself a particular course of action.

In the work place this is very much required. Let me show you why. Let's say you and I put our money together to open up a small business. This business will require much attention from both of us. To be more specific on this matter, you and I opened up a beauty salon and on the contract it is in detail that who does what and what percent each is to receive. My job is to make sure the equipment being used and sanitized after each use. I failed to do my job and the barber doesn't sanitize the blade after a cut. Why? Because he feels he can look at a customer and determine if they have a disease or something. The barber fails to do his job and the customer gets a staph infection or hepatitis in my shop. The both of us as owners are liable and opened for a lawsuit. This lawsuit can result in paying out a large sum of money plus medical bills.

We are barely making money to begin with. They will sue the partnership which means we are both liable. We aren't protected as an corporation because we are not one. This could have been avoided if only I would have been dedicated to the business relationship.

Pg.102

The act could destroy two relationships or maybe three. First, of all my partners might not want to be in business with me no more. He may feel it would be a better thing for him to move on and start another business with someone who will be dedicated. I have to understand that it's nothing personal. It's a business decision.

The barber I have working in the shop must be fired because what he caused. He must accept responsibility and understand and why he was terminated. This might be a barber who worked for us two years or fifty years. Now a relationship is destroyed.

A valuable customer may never return to the shop after coming for eighteen months continuously. That's another relationship destroyed and money lost. This may also cause a business shutdown if I can't find another business partner to continue with. Why? The reason is because I wasn't dedicated to my business. Do you understand how this is very important to have dedication?

Now, let's go into the millions of dollars. Let's say I invested $30,000,000 dollars in a gated community built on about two hundred acres of land. I hired someone to screen people to ensure no drugs or alcohol gets onto my property. There is excellent job performance for two years with no major incidents. There were nine drug busts within the two year period. The word gets out that you don't play any games and your security team is on top of everything. You may let your guards down. In your heart you feel the world has received your message of non-tolerance about drugs. So you don't screen people as you once started. Now one person slips in with a large amount of drugs. Then they pass the word that your guards are down. So six more people has slip by the guards with all kinds of drugs.

Two weeks pass and during those two weeks a certain group of people in their early twenties-who are going to college. They were the ones who slipped in my community with a lot of ecstasy pills. They party every night at one of the pool sightings and take the pills then freak out.

Now, let's say one morning comes and a woman in her late twenties comes with her two children one five and six years of age.

This is projected in the minds of people that are a safe drug free community. So the women get in the water with one of the kids and allow the other one to run around and play with a few other kids, who might be also at the pool with their parents. One of the kids finds four ecstasy pills, and eats them thinking its candy and two of the kids die.

Due to lack of dedication, where does that put my multi-million dollar business? First of all, I might go to prison. Then be sued which causes termination of my multi-million business. The reason is simple. Security wasn't dedicated from the point hired until the point. You decided to retire. Then on top of that, those are kids. To get these people in my community, they had to believe that they or their lives and their children's lives would not be in danger at all.

Dedication is serious. It could cause your life to be lost. It could cause your 3 year old child's life to be lost. Looking at this situation determine how many relationships are destroyed in this scenario.

2. Trust

When you trust someone you view them as honest, dependable and someone you confidence in.

In the work place this is important. Trust is another form of dedication. How is this true? When you are dedicated you are dependable. Even though it's a form of dedication, it's not pure dedication to the extreme. A person can be honest with you without being dedicated.

Example, a murder takes place in your front yard. You are the only eyewitness. It's in your yard so you are the first suspect. Now, you know that you are not about to go do life for something you didn't do. So when police arrives at your front door to ask you about it. An arrest will be made because you will tell them everything. Since you were honest to them but you were not dedicated to them at the same time.

You can't be dedicated to someone you don't have a relationship with. In a relationship, you must be trusted and dedicated to make it work. The relationship I'm referring to is the one in the work place. There must be trust, and I'm about to show you why.

Before I go out I need you to understand that when I say work place it's not limited to just working with someone. It also includes different sizes of businesses. Because rather you are a CEO or employee, you still have to trust the people you work for or with to some extent. I said to some extent because this isn't the same trust you render to your wife or husband.

Why is trust important?

Example One

Let's say I'm illiterate, but I have somehow come up on 60,000 dollars. The money was in receipt of someone's will to me after deductions. Being the well business minded man I am when I met you and you had no money to put in the business ideas. Your job only pays you anywhere between 600 to 900 dollars and after taxes and all of your bills are covered. You only have like $80.00 to buy some food. You found out that I have just come up on the $60,000 through word of mouth.

Then you approach me with this brilliant ideal to make over $200,000 using my money to invest. I immediately jump at the concept of increasing my money.

It was presented in this manner to me "Mr. Damond, sir after doing extensive research I have come up with a business plan to make you an extra 30,000 dollars, using your $60,000. Without knowing anything, I immediately get excited. All I was thinking about is an extra $30,000. I know nothing about percent or what you will make off the deal.

Common sense went out the door at the thought of my $60,000 becoming $90,000 and I don't have to do anything. He made $200,000 so I received $90,000 and received $110,000. I should have received more than him and I should have at least doubled my money and he received $80,000 but no, I trusted this man on this business deal and he wasn't to be trusted.

Example Two

We are both from the same neighborhood, slept in the same house, ate the same food, slept with the same females, went to the same school, and got into trouble together. We fought together and we were always with each other. We are now older and twenty one years of age. During our youth years you know we grew up rapping and singing in the hallway in the projects.

You had 100,000 dollars to invest and you decided to start a record label and put all four of us under it. Everyone is thinking the same, dog we grew up together, so we know Chris will not try to get over on us. So, we fully trust you to give us what you know we are supposed to have. Your love for money causes you to draw blood between us after all we been through. Why? We trusted you. The trust was a halfway issue. I felt played and much disrespected and you know me that I'm out of my mind at this point. I lived with the "I don't care attitude". So, I will kill you and your immediately family. Looking at this situation, many lives are taken because of your mistrust. You may not view it like that, but it's possible in this day in time.

Example Three

I opened up another kind of business and I hired you as my accountant. I trust you to not steal my money, but you do. You only take 1% every time because you feel I won't miss it. What you didn't know that without you even knowing. I had another accountant checking behind you.

This accountant got you stealing on record 1% for two years. She or he brought it to my attention and asked me to be cool because she might have made a mistake then it all comes out.

I bring it to you on record and let you go. Now by me being a major power position in the world, the media will get involved. Now the accountant name is out there as a thief which can cause issues for future employment. After all, why would a corporation want someone working for them who steal from them? You are forced to go back to a regular job. From there you have to drop all the expensive things you were used to do and live life from pay check to pay check. You again never get to do things above your means. Why? Because you refused to prove that you are trust worthy.

Deadly Trust

Example Four

Let's get a little more dangerous with this word trust. Let's say we are cool with each other. I have my own paint shop. In it I hired you to working inside of it painting vehicles. During the time you have worked there you know that I kept over $10,000 hid in the place.

One day I was closing and I was adding more money to my stash spot. Incidentally you saw me and you swore that you would not tell anyone about my spot. So I believed you.

Three weeks passed and you told someone thinking they wouldn't do or say anything. You didn't know that they would come to rob me. That time came and I was as usual closing up the shop, but this time as I added money to my stash spot. The guy you told came in with a gun and immediately told me to hand over the money. This was my lifesavings, my heart. So I refused to give him the money. He kills me and takes the money. I died behind you because I thought I could trust you and you gave me your word.

Some people would have said that I could have lived if I had given the money up. No! He was going to kill me anyway because I saw his face and we both knew each other. So my life is gone at the expense of your trust.

My wife is left to be a widow and my children are fatherless. Why? I didn't have the confidence in you. I thought I could at first, but I had to find out the hard way.

Deadly Trust continues

Example five

Now, let's take it to the Ghetto. What I'm about to talk about is really deadly ground. There is where we live on deadly ground. It's like at any moment someone could die. We were (are) like walking grave yards in the hood. At any given moment something can pop off and someone will get killed. All we have to do is throw a party or DJ and it's on. Let two guys who are beefing walk off in there and see each other. Then guns will begin to sound off, with over 40 shots being fired. I get killed and a sixteen year old girl is paralyzed for life. For what! I say a lot of foolishness which it is all the time. If you desire to know how we roll, act, live, breed, survive and really get down in the ghetto. I wrote another book that will give you in great detail our ten commandments. It's based on a true story (stories).

You are talking about Hollywood. Hollywood doesn't have anything on the people who lived and breed the heart of the streets. So, let me give you an example from the streets. This trust thing has to be exercised even on the streets of the ghetto. If not lives will be lost, children will be without parents, hearts of family members will be lost.

Based on a True Story

We both grew up together and I trust you because you took the fall for me when the police found drugs by my vehicle. You were the one who fought the guys who were too big for me to fight. We played catch which means to get a little bit with the young females. Hey man, we even played house with the girls next door. When our parents thought we were doing our homework together. By word of mouth you heard my aunt has $5000.

Your mind begins to ponder on how you could get it and how much you could do with $5000. The good side of you begins to remind you of all the good things we use to do. How my mother fed the both of us and both our parents go to church together? The evil side of you begins to plant thoughts telling you that you still could get the money and nobody gets hurt.

So you go to the project and find someone who will be down with you. You find a guy to roll with you but you let him know off the top that you have love for me and there will be no shooting. You farther tell him that my mother is a church going woman so this should be a piece of cake.

The two of you kick in the door at 2:00 a.m. in the morning. When you and the dude get in the house only my three little cousins are in there by themselves and the oldest is sixteen years of age. You wake them up and ask them where the money is. At this time, you not using common sense because who's going to tell a child where $5000 is in the house. You are only thinking about the money. So you get angry because your mind is telling you that these little girls, don't hurt them. So you decide to prove them wrong. You shot one and one pulled the mask off of your face. Now you have to kill all three of these little girls You know they know you, your mother and father and also where you live.

Then this puts you in a position you didn't anticipate from the get go. Bam! You shoot all three of them but the one you shot in the head didn't die.

In time you go to jail but you know I'm about handling my business. So I put all my family members on alert to not press charges.

So you can come home in sixty days. Then I catch you and it's all over for you.

3. Commitment

When you make the commitment to do something, you are making yourself obligated so you must do what you commit to. Yes, I trust you and I know you are very dedicated to being on time at work; but are you committed to the growth and expansion of the company?

Let's go to my favorite subject – the record label. I planned to have a major one in the future with me being the only CEO. Let's say I started my own record label. I opened it as a independent label, but set it up as a major label.

Yes it can be done all you need is the 2 C's capital and contact. My label won't be a major label at first but I will set it up as one. That way I could make noise as they make. Which means I will have a fully staff label. I will deal with the A & R (artist and repertoire) concerning commitment. Instead of having one or two as an independent label has, I will have a group of them, maybe made up of different groups-each specializing in different fields of music. That will be their only focus- the style of music they specialize in, etc.

Since I've just started and I have no artists but I have 15,000,000 dollars to begin with. The group of A & R is a part of the team I hired to work under my label. A part of my job is to find the artist and recommend to me that he be signed. After he or she is signed then you find out their style of music and assign those who specialize in it to them. Then they begin to work with the artist and seeing how he or she sound live, can they perform live, finding out do they write their own songs, and pushing the singles etc.

Now let's go back to the beginning. Your job is to find artists. What if in a 6 month period, you find no one you think is ready? What do I have to do then? After all, you commit to this, but now you are not carrying out your obligations. I was forced to get on you. I mean come on, let's look at the bright side. There is no such thing as you can't find anyone. There are more than enough unsigned people out there.

Going back a little, majority of the renowned artists in the industry came from the church choir. Some of them won at a talent show and some knew somebody there.

So what are you saying? As I write, there is a talent show going on right now. In every church in America, there is a choir with more than one lead singer. Better yet, go to one of those singing schools. Why should I have to tell you this? You know your occupation. Well then be committed to it and bring me some artists or my 15,000,000 dollars won't make me 150,000,000 dollars. If you are committed to the expansion of my label, you will bring several artists in and it wouldn't take you six months to do so. I'm talking about commitment.

Producer

We are still talking about this commitment thing. Yes, the producer is under my label and he has committed to his job at least that's what he told me. The job consists of helping the artist write songs id he can, he can get an artist signed to the label, and doing all the perfect things when it comes to the tracks. The CEO (me) and my producer agreed that he would have ten completed tracks for my new artist's cd in a certain period of time.

My label is in agreement with this. The personal manager had already approved of the songs the artist should record for this current time. The A & R is ready to push the singles as soon as possible. The sales department, new media, and international folks are ready and anticipating to push this new artist. These folks have put in in their schedule along with the other artists they have lined up.

The deadline has come and you only have three tracks recorded. First of all, I will be upset when I get the call that my artist's cd will have to be pushed back because the producer wasn't finished with doing the tracks. Now the label is looking at me to make sure this kind of things happens anymore. So, here I come and talk with you and you tell me that you forgot that your girl had a baby show and you had just moved in a new house but in actuality you were out whore hopping. Because you could have had ten baby showers, three funerals, and just moved in two houses. It shouldn't keep you from honoring your commitment.

You just got caught up in the moment and the time you thought you would stay with these whores lasted four months. Because every time they felt you were tired of them, they brought you two or three more girls.

I'm talking about commitment and you committed to this. Your commitment is catered to the growth and expansion of my new label. Without the sound, right sound, my label won't be around. So producer, before you sign under my label are you committed to what you obligated yourself to do?

I respect it more I you let me know upfront that you like to hang out and drink and pick up many women for pleasure. If this is your thing, don't let it interfere with your obligations to this label.

If you do, you are forcing my hand to let you go. I know you are a very good producer, but I run the show and just because you refused to be committed. I can't. I have committed to bringing my label to new heights. I will do what I have committed to do. Yes I know without sound I won't be around; but do you know that you're not the only producer in the world? When you sent your demo tape in, you just were the one picked. Now my money is involved. You either get your act together or I will have to let you go. I'm talking about being committed people. Your commitment can cause the rise or fall of a major operation.

Now let's talk about this commitment thing from another perspective – Prison. Just because someone is in prison doesn't mean that they are rightfully there and just because some is in prison doesn't mean that they can't change.

Now there are those will never or want to change. They will continue to do what they enjoy to do but always understand that everybody isn't and will never be the same.

Now don't think you really know about prison because you saw it on TV or what the media shows you. They only show you what can't really hurt them of the prisons. What I mean by hurt them, those who run the prison and steal the money.

I talk much about this raw and uncut in another book I wrote. I will just talk about it a little I like I said, you don't really know what really goes on until you experienced it firsthand. I did over 10 years in prison and you think I don't know what goes on inside. I'm not stupid, believe me when I tell you I lived and breed that life.

One of the things where I know they stole money is that when the faith base program was instituted in the prison where I'm doing time at. It only lasted about two years at first. I was in it.

Now let's use common sense. If I run a prison or I'm the governor, and the federal government give me money to start a program. I start the program and I don't build a building like I'm required to do. I use my own building. I don't pay individual to come in facilitate the program, and I don't purchase material to use in the program. Now I received the amount between 300,000 to 1 million to do this. I used my own property and use the people (church members and volunteers) who are already coming into the institution to facilitate it.

You answer the following question. How much money did it cost me? If it didn't cost me anything, where did the money go?

Here's another example, what if I, I'm a multimillionaire; I give you 300,000 dollars to build a new chapel for the inmates to worship God. Why would it take you over a year to build it? Then the only reason you started building it was because you heard I was coming to check on it to see how it's coming alone. So you hired one contractor who was already on contract with the prison and five inmates to begin building it.

I gave you 300,000. You won't pay the inmates. You will only increase their incentive pay to twenty cents (state money already).

What if you pay the company by the hour? The contractor probably was already paid. Then where did the money go? Better yet, I gave you my money. Why are you taking all of this?

You don't or didn't have to pay for? I deal with it more in the other book I just spoke about.

In prison you don't know how they beat us almost to death, hook us up to take our good time wrongfully, or how they feed us. The foods that will give us cancer in the long run, creating more bed space in the future.

Let's get back on this commitment thing. In prison, guards or security guards are put there to watch over us. So they have an obligation to something they have committed to doing. Answer this question? If you are committed to watching over me and making sure I'm safe which by the way they focus more on messing over us then protecting us. Why did my friend get his hand or head cut off by another inmate? Better yet, why did you allow that man to get raped? You say he's in here for raping a child, he deserves it. Regardless of what he is in here for. You still have a job to protect him. Because you weren't committed to your job I was raped.

Alright let's get off the child molester. Let's get on the drug dealer. The person that sells your daughter drugs on the streets. This same daughter, after she can't find a hit, steals her own baby's clothes and sells them for a hit. She also stole your new TV and she had sex with your new boyfriend for ten dollars.

Let's get on the drug dealer who gives her the drugs that makes her do all of these things. Now let's say I come to prison for drugs in prison you witness me and a dude that owe me money, and we immediately get in a fight. The guard broke the fight up and put us in the block. We get out the next day. By the way the block is the cell block, solitary confinement. In court we tell the people it's over and they believe us. So they put us back in the same dormitory. We both have killing on our minds. We are convicts who use to doing time. So we know how the ropes go. We know that if we tell the people we can't live with each other or we will do something to the other person. They won't put us together in population. So we tell them it is cool and we let the foolishness go.

So you all put us back together. We already understand what's up; whoever gets caught slipping it's all over. We will send him home before his release date in a box.

The time came, at night while everybody sleep. The dude got up and act like he was to use the bathroom, he stabbed me quickly twice in my heart without a struggle. He went right in the bathroom and cleaned the knife up. Then he came to the desk to talk to the desk to talk to the guard about two hours. As soon as you went to do your count, he slipped the knife in your bag. Now I'm dead and the killer got away. But the guard said you are committed to their job.

If the guard was committed, you would have watched the inmate from the time he got up to use the bathroom until he got back into his bed and I would still be living. My children wouldn't be fatherless, my parents heartbroken, and wife crushed. This all could have been avoided if you would have been committed.

4. Sacrifice

When you sacrifice you give up something that is of value to you for the sake of another that's more important or more worthy. How does sacrifice applies in the workplace?

It applies in the workplace and in the business field. Many people sacrifice quality time with their wife to pursue their goals in life. This could turn out good or bad. It depends totally upon the two people involved. Let's get into it!

Let's say I met this beautiful nice young female and we hit it off. We began to spend much time together. Then in time, after already understanding I'm in acting school, I receive within a three month period- five movie scripts which will take me at least four years to shoot.

Now you are cool with it at first. Then after the first movie is complete, you see how much time we are not spending anymore.

Now you have a problem with it. So you begin to complaint and tell me that we are not spending time as usual.

This is where the problem comes in. My dreams were already understood from the onset of our relationship. I understood you don't like to travel, but you still encouraged me to pursue my goals. The solution is simple-sacrifice. The woman obligated to sacrifice in this situation.

Because I encouraged her to travel with me so we could continue to spend more time together. She didn't want to because she valued her decision not to travel. She gave it up to be with me- someone more important than her decision not to travel. The result was we continued to do what we did to keep the relationship sweet.

Sacrifice in the work place. Let's say that the two of us work together. We have working together for ten years. So naturally we know each other's work assignment. So a time came while we were at work for me to sacrifice for you. I was scheduled to get off an hour before you, but something came up. Your son was hit by a car and you had to immediately leave to go see about him. Naturally I'm suppose to have an understanding. So you asked me to stay an extra hour for you and I did. Where did the sacrifice come in at? You didn't know that I and my wife had an appointment to meet up right after work. That's where the sacrifice came in. I gave up something that is of value to me for the sake of your son. My wife understood and was cool with the fact that I cared that much.

Now just think for a minute if the two of us had a half relationship. Half relationships are killers. If we had this I could have easily said "man I understand your problem, hut you know how women are. When you tell them that you will do something and you better do it."

That sounds good enough to be an excuse. The problem with that was I was lying. Because I'm married and I know my wife well enough to know that she isn't selfish or self-centered until the point where she would get upset over what I decided to do. You see, this is what a half relationship produces-half sacrifice.

What if I would have said no? Then the man would have had to stay at work because the position he has requires someone to be present until the shift changes. That would have crushed him. All types of thought would have been going through his head. One of them would have been killing me. Another one would have been; why are people so selfish? We didn't have a half relationship. Why? Because that type of relationship is a killer

5. Submission

When you submit to someone, you are being obedient to them. You can also submit in the work place or the business field, as a matter of fact, you must submit if you are working for someone or opening a business with someone.

The Work Place

Let's say you just were hired to work a job in a restaurant. Well naturally someone will be assigned to show you what you must do. Now for you to stay on the job, you must submit to their leadership.

So where does half submission play a part? You half submit when you listen but don't obey. Yes you can listen to their instruction but if you don't follow them something can go wrong then you are at fault. Why? Because you did what you wanted to do and not what you were instructed to do. If you do what you're instructed to do and something fails, then you're not at fault. When you deal in half relationships- half submission something will go wrong.

The Business Place

Let's say you and I become partners and open up a business. Now on the contracts it will be drawn out who do what. If I don't submit to what I have to do, then it's a breach of contract. The result will be the business will fail. Why? I was half submissive.

6. Communication

Communication is essential in the work place as well as in the relationship. You must have an understanding with the people you work with. This is what you gain by communication with them.

It doesn't have to be half-communication. It could be full, but limited. There is difference in limited communication and half-communication. The difference is you could fully communicated business wise, but limited the communication only to business.

7. Respect

The last one is respect. You and I could have jobs were we clean up areas right next to each other. Let's say I don't respect your area. I wait until you leave and act like a child and dirty your area up. Now let's say the boss had no understanding. So when he came to inspect our area. Yours was dirty. He calls you in and fired you. Why? I know because the inspection team came around to inspect the business area.

You didn't get fired because your area was dirty. You was fired because due to my half-respect. I respect you and your area when you were around, but when you wasn't around. I disrespected your area.

Now let's get off into intimate relationships.

CHAPTER 2 HALF RELATIONSHIPS

(In Intimate Relationships)

Now this is a killer in many, if not all relationships. I believe couples that are not fully committed to the relationship won't last. I don't believe it's in all relationships because in life you will always have some faithful people and you will have those who are not faithful. Always remember both individual involved must be on the same accord to make it last.

None Faithful

There are those who enter relationships and none plan on being faithful. Today that is called "Adult Relations."

I was in several of them. It was a time where I loved them. Because from the onset of the relation, it's already understood that there will be no strings attached. The ones I was involved in were just for sex. I never know them to involved nothing other than sex. Then most of the women were all from eight to eleven years older than me. I was only a teenager and they were in their twenties. I only wanted sex anyway. One of the ones I had was almost thirty years old but she looked as if she was 21. Her body was tight. As a matter of fact, everything about her was tight. She had thick legs, a pretty face and a nice physique. I didn't know her and she really didn't know me but when she seen me she wanted me. When I had seen her, the only thing I had on my mind was sex and I knew I wasn't going to be faithful.

In actuality, we both had the same thing on our mind sex. This is where none faithful come in at. She a boyfriend… I had a lot of girlfriends. She explained all of this to me, and told me that she doesn't care about all the women I had as long as she was number one. I was cool with that. We had sex that first night and which was an experience I will never forget.

It really didn't last long because she began to want a little too much. I was cool with sleeping over by her house to sex her, but she wanted me to lie up in the bed after sex. I wasn't with all that I understand now why women want that but when I was a teenager I wasn't with it.

Adult Relations

I had another female who wanted to do the same thing named Keisha. Keisha had two children, a girl and a boy. She had a job and her own house. She was fine but not all that pretty. She had good sex. She was 26 years old.

I met her through one of my friends. He's dead now. He and his girl were cool with the chick. So he and I went into her house and stayed about thirty minutes but I wasn't saying too much just sitting and laughing. So we would get up, leave and come back at the same time. So one of the times we got up to leave. She was like "why every time he gets up and leave you leave. What you afraid someone will do you something?"

Now I could have argued the point, telling her that she doesn't know me to stay up in her house like that. I didn't because I knew she wanted to see what's up with me. I saw through it so I stayed there and we begin to talk and get to know each other. After he left she offered me some marijuana and she was already high. Sex wasn't even on my mind until she told me I could sleep over. Then I knew then what she wanted to do. So, I went along with the flow. I ended up sleeping by her house and sexing her. She didn't want to do it because she didn't want me to think she was a whore. She still gave it up. The next morning I got up before the sun came up and went home. I never came back so she sent for me. I went to see her and talked to me and was wondering why I never came back. Then she let me know I could come over by her whenever I wanted to.

I never found time to do so because I had another one the same age but more sexier and prettier. She had a light skin complexion which I loved but they were the same age.

The first time, we wore protection. The second time I didn't have to. We both got what we wanted-great sex. After the second time, she still wanted me to come back the next night. This is what she told me. I didn't come back. It wasn't that I didn't want to. I just had too many females to sex to keep my focus only on her. She had to catch me at the right time. Because once I laid it down good on her. I knew I could come back and get that. They always wanted me to come back.

A Caring Motive or Deceptive One

When I went to prison I met this white young fine chick. She was in a relationship with my friend and I was writing her lil sister in college. She was a prison guard. I and her lil sister were on a positive level. We were on a just kicking it level at first.

Through much talking she begins to know about my talents. On top of that we use to sing to each other. She was afraid to sing in front of people but not me. She had a beautiful voice. In time, we got on another level, freaky level. She explained to me about that ,but I changed her mind and made her give me the conversation I wanted.

She wasn't comfortable because I was writing her sister and she was dating my friend so what I did, I got on a freaky subject that caters to her. She was all smiles. I begin to talk to her about oral sex. I told her if I ever commit oral sex on a woman it had to be a white girl. She asked me why I told her because her vagina is pretty. She started laughing but she took the bait.

Then she begins to teach me how to eat a woman's vagina the right way. She was telling me what to do with fingers and my tongue. I was getting hot. Did I ever do it? No! And I'm never going to do it.

Now after that it wasn't long before she started writing me freaky letters about how she would sex me.

The reason I brought Wendy up was because she told me that she wanted to get into an adult relationship with me. She knew I would someday become rich and famous. So we talked about it one day.

We talked about females who will try to have sex with me, then try to sue me. So to avoid that, if I don't find a female to be on my team, she will be there to sex me anytime I wanted to.

I was cool with it. She stopped messing with my dude because of something he did. I tried and tried to keep them together but he did something that he couldn't take back. When it came to sex with her, I act as if I didn't know much. So her imagination begins to run wild thinking of ways to sex me. Little did she know that I was very experienced?

Now she wanted to sex me. Do you think it was for the money or because she just wanted to? I think and know she is the type of female who play games with inmate's mind. I know how she thinks and she couldn't play with my mind. I'm the type of person who would make you think you running game, but I would be in control all the time.

Now let's get into the half relationships with dedication, trust, commitment, sacrifice, submission, communication, and respect. Then I will talk about the best relationship to be in.

1. **Dedication**

When you dedicate yourself to someone, you set them apart for special use. You are dedicated to them.

Dedication is very important in a relationship. It is one of the keys to a good relationship. This I will deal with in the next chapter. Now I will deal half dedication.

Example One

The first example of a half dedication is when one in the relationship is dedicated and the other is not. You see this all the time when women are seen in a relationship pushing me to do certain things that they know they should do.

Let's say just ministering to her emotions by telling her he loves her or she is beautiful or I need you baby. She is dedicated to telling you things of that nature, but you feel it's not important enough to tell her that. What you must know is that it's not all about you no more- it's about the both of you. So, if you continue to not cater to her emotions, you are operating in half dedication.

Example Two

Let's deal on the children's level. Let's say you and your wife agrees that you (the man) or the one who takes the school shopping the week before they go to school.

Now, this is already understood by the both of you. So no one has to say anything to the other about what to do. The time came and you forgot. So when the day came for them to go to school. They had no clothes to go to school. This causes an argument between you and your wife. The reason was because you were half dedicated, and half dedication just won't get it. Yes, it may be small to you but it's not small. Your relationship with your wife or girl gets under the fire.

Example Three

Let's say you and I as a couple agree to sit down with one another and assess out relationship. The two of us agree to what would cause our love to weaken. Now, we are in love but we want to grow more and more in love. In the time that we developed this love we discovered each other's dislikes. So, we know the buttons to push on each other.

This isn't right at all, any in a playing manner.

A Playing Motive Builds Destructive Killers

A playing motive builds destructive killers. These two killers are resentment and half dedication.

You are already half dedicating when you do this. Let me show you how. When you know what not to do because you're doing begins a separation between you and your spouse and still do it. You cultivate the half dedication. This will end in a split if you don't stop.

Now let's get specific! Let's say we are in a relationship. In time I found out that you don't like when I stare at other women. Let's say always stare at other women, especially when she is with me. This will build an inner resentment in her. I am half dedicated because I am refusing to do what I know will keep the relationship right. When I look at other women constantly like that to her I'm saying that I'm not satisfied or I'm not happy with what I have. So when you continue to do this. You are half dedicating yourself. This is a killer in the relationship. Because resentment is constantly on the rise, soon or later she will get tired of it and separate from you. It's not that she wants to you are forcing her to.

Why? She wants to live with you in peace. You aren't helping any. You are living in half-dedication. This leads to separation.

Now let's say that I'm the woman and my husband or boyfriend tells or rather express to me that he don't like when I express a renowned superstar to be my future husband or my baby. I being a woman am saying several things there. I could be playing outwardly but serious inwardly. My seriousness may be manifest by getting pictures of this guy and hang them up in my house. So, I could just look into his face and maybe his body to in a lustful way. Every time I give my attention to these pictures, I am giving and building affection for someone I don't even know. As I continue to pay them attention it grows and grows. When I say that's my baby. What I am saying is that I'm in love with my husband and I desire to fall in love with another man.

In my mind, I secretly had long to be sexed by that man. And if time ever presented it, I would immediately let that man sex me and try my best not to let my husband find out. If he does, I would cry and ask him to forgive me. It's a great possibility that he won't find out the man being a superstar in all.

Now if my husband finds out and we separate, it's my entire fault. I have no one to blame but myself. I had a good relationship but my half dedication destroyed it. When I said that the person is my future husband, what I am saying is that I will let my now husband go. When I met this superstar and he wanted to be with me.

In front of my boyfriend, I am playing, but in my heart I'm serious. He told me that he doesn't like it and I still do it. What I'm doing I'm disregarding his feelings, being half dedicated and building resentment in him toward me and the man I'm secretly loving on, rather infatuated with. I told you a playing motive builds destructive killers. Those killers are resentment and half dedication.

Why would I want to continue to live and love someone who continues to cause me to be very resentful to them? I want to love him or her but they are driving me away.

My boyfriend/girlfriend is supposed to be my baby and future spouse. If this is not what you do or feel, it weakens the relationship. This is half dedication and it destroys something so beautiful – love. I deal more with this "So you want to play Games."

Constructive Criticism verses Destructive Criticism

Constructive Criticism

This is a tool used to push an individual forward although the one being criticized doesn't always feel this way. It is for that purpose only.

Let's say you and I am a couple, I'm your husband and you are my wife. By this time that we are married, we know each other's goals and abilities in life. Now say you are an artist and the music you sing caters to only one genre of people. So every time you drop a CD it always sells around the same amount of units. Understanding the industry and good marketing strategies, I sit you down and talk to you about it and being your husband in all.

Let's say you only sing gospel music and you are a devoted Christian. What are you taught in your church is that you have to sing only Gospel music or you are going to hell. You believe this and you are scared to death to sing about any other thing but the death burial and resurrection of Jesus Christ. This is the belief of the Christian faith.

Now say I come along and tell you different. Somewhere around these lines, "baby you will never sell a million copies because you only have a certain fan base. You talk about the same things baby." She may think I don't believe in her which is not true. Or she may feel that I'm criticizing her talent, destructive criticism.

Now what I'm trying to do is get you to do what you are doing in a different way or style. This will be the only way you can and will get different results. So, I sit you down again. Why again? Because when I told you that you won't go platinum you was ready to take my head off. So I sat you down again. I said baby let's look at your field. You sing gospel music and you have fans and other people who sing gospel music have fans. Now just because people buy this gospel artist's music doesn't mean they will buy yours. This is not to say that they don't like you. They might not like your style of singing. They might not like your voice anything could be the reason.

Then I tell you or rather explain to you what I know to do to sell more than a million copies. First, I captivate your mind by telling you my tragedy. I know its good music to your ears.

Then we examine the spiritual industry. We find out that in this field alone there are different kinds of people who like different kinds of music. We discovered in this field we have people who like traditional Gospel, Gospel music, Praise music, Worship music, Christian Rock, Country Gospel, and Gospel Rap/Hip Hop.

So what we do now? In order to reach these different people I must sing their style of music. So what I do is mix my CDs up from then on. I make hits for at least half of not all. Then I would be creating new markets. You can also add what I call universal message-love music.

I know you might be saying "oh Lord he trying to send me to hell now?" No I'm not! Love was created by God. So it's spiritual. It's not Gospel music, but is spiritual music. So if God ordained for a man and woman to be in love. Why is it wrong to sing about love?

Now let's take your bible and it will reveal truth. This is what you believe right? This is your Christian faith right? So if it's in the bible it's good. If it's in harmony with scripture, you won't go to hell right?

Okay, they have scriptures in the bible showing you how to love your spouse. If you get behind the pulpit and preach those scriptures, is it right or wrong? It's right? Take these same scriptures and sing them. You have a gift to sing. You can't preach. So your way of ministering to people is through music. Are you wrong? No, because you are in harmony with your bible.

Now when you sing a song that's contrary to your bible, then you have to worry about sinning against God. Say you sing or write a song that encourages people to commit adultery. Then you are out of harmony with your bible.

So my point in this all is that you mix your CDs up if you want to sell more copies and you still could be in line with your faith. This is constructive criticism. I know it could lead you to improve your craft. When I do this I am not saying I don't believe in you. I want to see you happy and succeed in life. I know you are upset when you sell under a million copies. So I will show you how to do it. If that's not saying I want you to succeed in life, I don't know what is.

Another example of constructive criticism is when you are my husband and I am your wife. You know my craft is singing. You know I can sing but I don't know how to sing there is a difference.

I can have the gift to sing, but the gift was never perfected. So in my house my husband loves to hear me sing. This caters to my ego until the point that I feel I am ready to pursue a singing career. So I rushed with excitement to my husband to tell him that.

He tells me something that breaks my spirit. It crushes me to the point where I no longer want to sing even in the house. He told me that I'm not ready to pursue a record deal. I interpret it as he is saying that I can't sing, but he isn't.

Then my husband being wise not only tells me but he shows me that I'm not ready to pursue a music career.

First, you in love explain to me my short comings. You tell me I'm tune def. I argue the point. So, you sit me down in our living room and put the radio on and allow me to listen to a familiar song. Then you turn the radio off and tell me to sing that song in the same key and how it was sung.

You start off right but throughout the song you sing out of key plus you sing flat. In your mind you sing the song which you did, but you didn't sing it right.

I'm showing you this to help you improve in those areas. If I didn't love you I would have told you to go on and sing before a manager or producer. And they crush you even harder then you felt when I told you that. I love you. I'm showing you how a singing coach will deal with you. They won't focus on telling you what you can't do. They will show you how it's done. You only have to listen and follow their lead like I wanted you to do.

CHAPTER 3
Half Relationships (In Intimate Relationships) Part 2

In order for me to tell you something about your voice, I have to know what I'm talking about. Not only that, I must be able to show you the way it's done. Because I know how it's done.

This is constructive because I am giving you tools to improve your craft. If I know these things and refuse to tell you this, I'm half dedicating myself to you.

Now, let's look at destructive criticism.

Destructive Criticism

This is when you are constantly telling your spouse that he or she will never be anything. No matter how hard you try, you will never amount to nothing in life. You are stupid. You can't do this or that. I don't even know why you were put here.

Many individuals don't understand how powerful words are and they are the reason many of our children are out of control. I was one of those kids. I will deal with this in the next part of this book when I deal with the family.

2. Trust

Complete trust in a relationship is vital to its longevity. Half trust only weakens the relationship. Which can so end it?

Example 1

Let's say me and you are married. We have been together for five years now. Now let's say me and you go out to have a good time. Now I go away to use the restroom, in the process this guy begins to talk to you. I can see this from a distance but I don't approach the two of you. I wait until he walks off then I come and start an argument with you, asking you why you are talking to another man. I argue this as if it's wrong for you to talk to other men.

What am I showing is half-trust? I don't bother to ask what the two of you are talking about. I just assume he was hitting on you. Which he was but you handled the situation right letting him know you are happy with the man you are with and you're not going anywhere. Half-trust causes arguments. These arguments will hurt the relationship if they are continued.

Example 2

Let's say my wife works in an office building which has 80% men and 20% women. In this building you have men who are very immature. One of them tries to get close to my girl after knowing that she is in a relationship. He may feed her the saying.

That no one will find out. She tells him off. This causes him to put a rumor out that the two of them slept together. The rumor hurts my wife until the points she cries. She cries because people believe it. She doesn't tell me because she wants to protect me.

In her mind she hopes I trust her enough to not believe it. The rumor hurts her but it's even more hurtful to the thought of me believing in this.

She didn't tell me because she knew I would go and really deal with that guy. She feels it would get out of hand until the point one of us end up dead and the other in prison for life. So in her love for me she suffers emotionally. This is how much she loves me. Now if I hear about the rumor and I believe it. I confront her with it. I'm not worried and care about her emotional pain right now. My only concern is that she cheated on me. I'm not concerned about how she feels.

So now my half trust builds on her already painful heart and mind. I don't understand that the fact that her husband doesn't trust her breaks her down even more.

I revealed the key to make this work in the next chapter. I revealed how to handle this in a way to improve and not destroy the relationship. I showed my half-trust by approaching you about the situation. I may say I trust you but I showed different with my approach. So you see what half-trust does? It separates the two of you. This is not good for the relationship. It's a killer that will kill.

Example 3

It could be the other way around. Let's say the man is in a situation with a woman and the situation goes as follows. I work around this woman who is very seductive and very beautiful. Now her thing is that she sexes all men who have something going for themselves. I'm not the one to tell my wife since I know how she will react when she finds out. Under this kind of atmosphere at wife only understands and believes all men will cheat. This is what society feeds to her. So she don' think through the whole situation. She lets her emotions block out her reasoning ability. She tells me to leave the job but she's not thinking about how I been at this company for ten years. She reveals her half-trust of me by telling me that. She believes society over me. So in an effort to save her marriage she tells me to leave the job.

If I don't quit the job, she is coming to get on the females case. Why? She doesn't fully trust me. Now me, I'm a man. So I', attracted to the female and I get thoughts in my head about how good the sex might be. Around this woman, my nature rises. She sees and knows this, so she continues her seduction. The truth is that I never touch the woman. I don't cheat even though I am attracted to the woman. If my girl begins to accuse me, it may be the push I need.

Let's say she accuse me from the point where she really believes I cheated. One day I came home and she wanted sex and I wasn't in the mood. This really sealed her belief. Now no matter what I say to her I still had sex with that woman. Now she is mad for two months. In those two months, she got tempted and had sex with another man because in her mind this will make the situation right, which never does.

First of all, I didn't sleep with the other woman. I tried to explain that the reason I didn't sleep with her at the time because the woman was on my mind. In the bed, I would have been thinking about the woman. She should have understood this but because she didn't. Now I'm about to leave because she slept with another man. I didn't and will never do so but because you didn't completely trust me. Now we are separated.

I told you half trust is a killer that will kill. You need not to half trust. If you do, you will be sorry in the end.

I will say many people live with the connotation that you have to enter a relationship with someone and they have to earn your trust.

This is, as is with dedication, sacrifice, respect, commitment; submission and communication must be presented in the beginning of the relationship.

When you enter the relationship, these things must be exercised from the start. Trust is not the same as love. You can't love someone the same day you meet them, unless it's with God's love. We are talking about Eros the love between a man and a woman. Now you have to trust them in the beginning of the relationship. I will show you how simple this trust thing is in the next chapter.

3. Commitment

When you are committed you are involving yourself in an obligation. We are dealing with half commitment, not true commitment yet. True commitment will be dealt with in the next

Example 1

Let's say my name is Keoshia and I'm a 30 year old short, fine, beautiful young lady. Let's say I meet you in the mall shopping for your little girl. I am shopping for my little girl also. We bump heads and hit it off.

Now I'm a woman. I'm the type that puts my all in every relationship I enter. I don't care if I were hurt once or twice. I truly understand that to make this work. I must be true on the commitment level to my man. I refuse to let a pass experience stop me from loving and being free. So I enter this relationship with total commitment on my mind but you don't. You and I agreed that we will be committed to making this relationship work. What are we saying is that we are obligating ourselves to the growth of this relationship?

Take something simple as holding me before the two of us have sex. I'm a woman I need this. When we first entered the relationship I let you know I need to be hold. At first you agreed to it because you only had sex on your mind. But I sometimes just want to be held tightly. I like to take a shower with you baby but we don't have to have sex every time. Sometimes I just want you to wash my body and you wash mines. Now say the man does this but he complains about it in the process.

This is half commitment. The woman will soon get tired of your complaints and she won't ask you to do this. She still loves you but want to live with you in peace. Now do you know what you did? You are putting her in the danger zone. Let me say it this way, your half commitment is putting her in a danger zone.

When you do this you leave the door open for me to move in. your woman is not being fulfilled. Something simple as this means more than sex to her.

Now sex means a lot to the man. So she gives it to him. He doesn't give her what she needs.

So a man, another man sits back and watches this. It's also dangerous for a woman to talk to outsiders about her husband. And for a woman to talk to her friends or people about what her husband is not doing.

The wrong ears could hear this and it than becomes the opening door for him to move into the situation. What do you think will happen if he can provide her with this? She is very tempted. Some women fall for it, and some stay true to the man they love even though unfulfilled. This could be avoided if you were fully committed. I will go into in the next chapter.

Example 2

I'm still the woman right now. Now let's say it this way. This is a common thing. I will deal with what men love-sex. Women love sex too, they just could hold out longer than some men.

We are committed to meet each other's sexual needs. If not, this is half commitment Now let's say you are an actor. You leave me at home while you film a nine month movie. I'm in New Orleans and you are in New York. We talk over the phone and I express to you that I need to make love but you tell me that you are in an important part of the movie and you have to relocate. I understand you but you don't understand I need you to make love to me. This is something you are supposed to know already. You put her in the danger zone. She is tempted and the man maid looking real good right now.

So what we being a woman does at this moment I make myself available. I'm thinking that you will be out of town eight more months. So I incidentally put myself on the maid. I'm not thinking about you or what we have built together. My vagina is thinking for me. It's telling me that good sex is what I need. Now not all women do this but you are not supposed to put a woman into this kind of situation at all. This could be avoided if you weren't half committed.

Now the maid got your goods. Now when you call home I'm not rushing you to come home sooner because the maid (male) gave me a sexual experience I will never forget. He won't say anything because he is afraid he will lose his job.

What's the reason for all of this? It's the killer in a relationship half commitment. The next chapter reveals the cure for this. This will save your relationship.

4. Sacrifice

I must say this before I go on. This book is really challenging my mind because I have never been in a true relationship the 28 years on my life on this earth, but when I got a little older I fell in love.

Now let's deal with this sacrifice thing. When you sacrifice for your love one, you give up a special thing you love to do to please or fulfill them. This is half sacrifice. It's when you are put into a situation to sacrifice but don't do it.

Let's day we live together and are barely making it. We both have a job and together we pay the bills and supply the food. After we are finish paying the bills we both have a little something left over. As time goes by, I being the man loses my job and it's had to find another one. So this means the little money we had left over have to go toward the bills until I could find a job.

I give my money up but you are hook to the casino. This is where all of your money goes. So you refuse to. I'm broke. I put up all the money I had saved up. You had no money because every time we split the left overs. You go straight to the casino. Now the time comes when you really have to sacrifice to keep us in a home and out relationship right.

You don't win. So now you come home to a house without lights and water because we only had enough to keep a roof over our head. Then on top of that a very upset husband. This is what your half sacrifice caused. Now I'm thinking about leaving because I feel you love the machines more than you love me. You care more about rolling dice than your husband drinking a cold glass of water. It's time for me to think about if you will begin to steal from me to appease your habit. I love you but I'm scare to death of what you are capable of doing now.

Do you now see how dangerous half-sacrifice causes many problems?

5. <u>Submission</u>

To submit means to obey someone's instructions. You half submit when you don't obey. Let's say you and I am a couple. I'm the man and you are the woman. Now say I see how men play and love to talk and be around you. You let me know that they are just friends and you have a lot of friends. I believe nothing is wrong with that but lines have to be set even with them. Now being a man and know how men think. You being a woman and know how women think. Now say I entered into a relationship with empathy and you don't.

Now let's say I have this female who you see is trying to get me to sex her. You can tell how she looks at me and acts around me. So you tell me about it and I listen. I go to the female and let her know if you want to remain friends with me. You have to stop touching me in my face, hitting me on my back side and bumping up into me trying to get me hot. You say that you are playing but my girl told me different. I submitted to her and stopped her from doing this.

Now it's your turn! You play with these guys you view as your friends and you both harmlessly bump up against each other every now and again. I know he's getting hot but you say you won't fall for him. You can control yourself. This is half submission. It's a killer. Do you think I want another woman who lets another man touch on her body?

You told me not to let that woman touch on my body. Is it alright for you because you can handle it? No! I don't work like that baby girl. So keep reading I will show you how it work in "The best relationship to be in." I keep telling you it's not about you no more. It's about you both the two of you. If something isn't right with one, the other has to get it right.

Example 2

Let's say you are my girl and I'm your boyfriend. You have a good job making good money. I work on the street selling drugs.

Now when you met me you knew what I did but you also believed I would change if only someone who really cares pushes me to showing me that here is a better way.

Now everything I ever told me to do you did it knowing and understanding that it is only for the better of you.

On my end, I listened to you until you told me to give up something I really love. I love selling drugs. I mean this all I know. I can't get a job. I just was released from prison.

You show me a different way to make money the right way. In the process of this, you continue to push me to play basketball because you know I'm the hottest player every time I touch a court. I don't listen and I only want to make easy money and sex your beautiful body. So in time you get pregnant and I go to jail. Now let's look at what my half submission caused.

First of all, I'm on parole this is my third drug conviction and I was caught with the drugs. Now what do you think will happen? I left my girl with more problems and pressured. She has to pay all the bills, work while she's pregnant and then take of me. I put more pressure on her accusing her of sleeping with another man, getting me a lawyer and keeping money in my account. Then on top of that I want mail and visits. My girl has no problems with this but here is where the problem arises.

I received 15 years for my drug charge. Now say I have to do half. In this atmosphere your girl has been sexed by about five different men. Your son is being raised by someone who might don't even give a care about him and your life was pushed back. Why? I believe it was your half submission. Keep reading to learn what could have happened to this guy in 7 ½ years.

In this situation I can't get upset and I put my girl in it. My half submission caused all of this.

6. <u>Communication</u>

Communication is always a two way thing. Remember the woman who wasn't getting hold when she needed? Well that's a form of communication. In communication both parties involved must receive understanding for it to be communication.

Half communication also is a killer. It causes curiosity to emerge, producing doubt and distrust. Half communication is when you refuse your spouse of sex, quality time and the right to know.

Sex

It's a form of communication. The person who refuses to give it willingly, the other is tempted to go elsewhere. Why? you are half communication with them. If they have sex with someone else whose fault is that? I don't agree with this but you are the cause of it.

Quality Time

You don't have to spend all of your time with your spouse but the two of you must spend time to grow. If one is willing and the other is not willing or available this is half communication.

The Right to Know

This is a very broad statement. She has a right to know you in and out. She shouldn't have to ask you. This is communication at its finest at this level; body language becomes a form of communication. Half communication prevents all of this.

7. Respect

When you beat on a woman you are half respecting her. You are disrespecting her. Whenever you kiss, sex or touch another woman. You are disrespecting her. This is half respect. Whenever you kiss or sex or touch another man you are half respecting your husband or boyfriend. This is a killer.

What if I caught you committing oral sex on another man because I told you I don't like that? So you went and did it to another man. Then I beat on you.

For the record, I would never put my hands on a woman to hurt her. We both wrong. We both disrespect each other. Half respect caused all of this. Half respect is when you sit in the house and watch porn when you have a wife at home.

What you are saying is that she is not enough. Half respect is when the woman sits and lust off of sexy men on TV when she has a man at home. This is disrespect and will soon cause problems if you keep giving your attention and affections to another man. Now let's get into the relationship that works and last.

CHAPTER 4 The Best Relationship to be in (Keys That Unlock the Road to a Lasting Intimate Relationship)

This is my favorite chapter. I couldn't wait to reach this point. I used the word keys because it represents authority. When you have the key to something, you have the power to open and close the ways to the other side of it.

You have something that completes or holds together the part of another thing. I want you to get this now. I said before, relationships don't fail people fail.

People fail in their own relationships because they don't use the keys that they have to have to hold it together.

Let's get started.

I said before that you grow in love. It's a beautiful process. The key to the beginning of it is about mind control. Not controlling the mind of no one else but controlling yours. This is to say that you have just left an abusive relationship.

When you are about to enter a new relationship, the first thing you must do is remember that this is a new beginning for you. A fresh start! Put this in your mind that you have never been hurt, beaten or bruised. In addition to this, that all men are not the same or all women. Men want to be loved just like women do.

Honey, trust, commitment, dedication, communication, sacrifice, submission, and respect must be exercised from the onset of the relationship. This will evolve into the last key -love.

In the previous chapter you were taught what half trust, commitment, dedication, sacrifice, submission and respect leads to. So if you want problems in this relationship circle, then do the half way thing. If you want a relationship that last until death due the two apart then the both of you-the man and the woman, you have to enter it the same way with your minds on the same accord.

Let's get deeper!

1. Dedication

When you are dedicated to someone, you devote your time and energy to them.

The book writer dedicates his time to completing a beautiful master piece. The songwriter dedicates himself to his craft because this is becoming of him.

When you dedicate yourself to someone, you are concerned about their well-being. What you do for or around them never hurts them. If my wife or girlfriend gets upset with me because I look at another woman like I look at them. I should never do this again, vice versa. This is complete dedication.

I deal with the power of affection in another place. You could try to justify your actions but later on down the line don't wonder why the two of you aren't getting along or why you are losing interest in your wife. It's simple you stepped out of the proper environment outlines in chapter 2 and whenever you do so you will begin to die off in your relationship.

You must dedicate yourself to her love only. This means in the beginning until the end. In the beginning before you mad love to her. You gave her all of your affection so continue to do the same.

Dedicate yourself to falling in affection with her over and over again. You must keep her with your full attention. Take those pictures of other women rather celebrities or not- and throw them away. In place of them put pictures of your mate up. This is your superstar, if you fell out of love; rekindle that attraction just like you ignite something paying attention to another woman.

When you meet her, you are supposed to dedicate yourself to her mind, body, and soul.

If she has a recurring problem at work, she needs sympathy. She wants you to commiserate her. She isn't seeking a solution to the problem. So don't give her any. She needs consolation. If she is sick, you take care of her until she gets well. That means to wait on her hand and foot. You also contribute to everything that needs to be done in the house. This is total dedication, a key to a great and lasting relationship. Both parties have to exercise it.

2. Communication

Complete communication is what makes the relationship last. Communication can take place in different forms: sex, words, body contact, and body language. In this part I will deal with barriers to effective communication.

Sex

People have different preferences about everything. So to disagree about sex is normal to do (Laumann et al., 1994).

My advice is this. If you are in a relationship with someone and don't know how they liked to get pleased sexually. You best find out, it will lead to them being frustrated and unsatisfied.

My belief should be everyone's belief if they want a lasting relationship. I deal with sex in another part but I want to ask you a question. If oral and anal sex is a natural affection, why do we begin to desire other sex partners in our bed?

Why does it lead to us being unfaithful in our relationship? I'll tell you why, because it is not God's plan. When you do this you enter an environment that's not God's design. Changing your mate won't do a thing. You will get tired of the next mate also. Your problem is self-control and leaving God out your sex bed.

As long as you think that it is not. I promise you that every relationship you enter won't last in faithfulness. You will still be frustrated and unsatisfied because you can't satisfy an uncontrolled lustful spirit. Yu have to practice self-control in the sex bed. There is no way around it.

Control yourself or you'll never be in a peaceful relationship.

Deadly Affects

God ordained sex between a woman and a man (Genesis 1:28). You can't be fruitful engaging in anal and oral sex but what you can do is slowly destroy yourself.

Psychologist agrees that a positive aspect of oral sex is that it doesn't result in pregnancy. God isn't against children. Each child born in the process of time will be a defense, support, and propagation of God's external plan on earth (Psalms 127:3.4).

It's possible to contract some sexually transmitted diseases through mouth-genital stimulation, especially when sperm is swallowed in fellatio. AIDS is easily transmitted by anal sex as rectal tissues are easily torn. This allows the virus to pass through the membrane.

Ask yourself a serious question? Would a loving God allow engaging in activities that lead to you contracting a disease that will kill you? This is why you are to have one mate and engage in his plan for the sex bed. I know is vaginal intercourse only in the environment of self-control.

This is why I said what I said earlier. Know your sex partner preferences. If she likes oral sex and you don't perform it, then its best you not enter that relationship. The reason is simple. She won't be satisfying either way because she is operating in the environment of lust. I talk about this next.

She may agree to still be with you for security reasons but she still longs for a vagina licked. So this presents the temptation to cheat because every man is tempted when he or she is drawn away by their own longing (James1:14). She may not cheat right off but if you make her mad. She will act off of emotions and do what she had in her heart to do all along. Then it was with that same guy she kept around that she heard him say how good he is with his tongue. So don' be like most individuals feeling uncomfortable telling your mate what you want sexually (Hatfield & Rapson, 1996). You should know up front.

There are several reasons people pursue extramarital sexual encounter. One is as I said before anger toward a partner, dissatisfaction (Thompson, 1983), desire for new and different sexual experiences (Buunk, 1980).

All of which comes from uncontrolled desires.

The Environment of Lust

Let's go back to Genesis 1:28. God told our parents Adam and Eve to be fruitful and multiply. The Hebrew word for fruitful is paw-raw, and it means to bring forth fruit, in our case this is children. The only way to do so is through vaginal penetration. This is the pleasure of sex. Yes we must enjoy it, but any other way is an unnatural affection.

Jesus said that whoever looks at a woman to lust after her is guilty of physical adultery (Matthew 5:28). The Greek word for lust is "epee thoo meho" and it means to set the heart upon that is long for.

When you operate in the environment of lust you practice anal, oral sex, masturbation, rapes takes place, unfaithfulness. Women start fantasying about threesomes, foursomes. They flirt with different men because lust can't be satisfied.

Let me show you how bad flirting is. Many rapes take place as a result of women leading men on for attention (Lim & Roloff, 1999). They tease men without wanting them to have sexual intercourse with them (Gillen & Muncher, 1995). This is all the environment of lust and an example of an unsatisfied individual.

In time pornography enters the picture and during all of these indulgence inside you are dying because that void will never be filled outside of God's plan for the sex bed.

This is why men can't fall in love with men. Because it's an unnatural affection (Romans1:27). It's a strong passion motivated by an evil spirit. It's excitement of the mind not the heart. Love deals in the heart.

What is the cure? The same as I said before self-control.

When you have this you control your emotions, desires, and actions. When do you do this, you do it throughout your whole life in every area of your life. You will enjoy peace, faithfulness and the longevity of a lasting relationship, when you do so.

Be the one who knows it all, and refuse to but you're only hurting yourself. Don't wonder why you are so miserable inside and all the methods you tried didn't work. I told you before you tried them.

Words

Words have a powerful impact on how we perceive and feel about the ones we hear (Proverbs518:21). When you are communicating with your mate, it is best to select the right words to say to them. This is because of the power they carry.

When you communicate with them, listen also to them. Open communication dispels all curiosity. Doubts then should never enter the mind. Trust is strengthening.

When you go through this, the two of you will grow together the both of you understand each other. This will increase your communication level on the word level.

This type of communication involves real dedication. I know sometimes you might not want to listen to your mate.

Effective Listening

The following is taken from the book, Psychology applied to modern life.

"To be a good listener, you need to keep four points in mind."

1)." <u>Communicate your interest in the speaker by using nonverbal cues.</u> Face the speaker squarely and lean toward him or her (rather than slouching or leaning back in a chair).

This posture sends a clear nonverbal message that you are interested in what the other person has to say. Try not to cross your arms and legs, as this posture can signal defensiveness.

Maintaining eye contact with the speaker also indicates your attentiveness. Communicate your feelings about what the speaker is saying by nodding your head or raising your eyebrows.

2). <u>Hear the other person out before you respond.</u> Listeners often tune out or interrupt a conversational partner when (1) they know someone well (because they believe that they already know what the speaker will say). (2). A speaker had mannerism listeners find frustrating (stuttering, mumbling, speaking in a monotone), and (3) a speaker discusses ideas (abortion) that generate strong feelings or uses terms (welfare cheat, redneck) that push "red buttons" (Verderber and Verderber, 2001).

3). <u>Engage in active listening</u> (Mckay et al., 1995). Pay careful attention to what the speaker is saying and mindfully process the information. Active listening also involves the skills of clarifying and paraphrasing. Inevitably, a speaker will ship over an essential point or say something that is confusing. When this happens, you need to ask for clarification. "Was Bill her boyfriend or her brother?" Clarifying ensures that you have an accurate picture of the message and tells the speaker that you are interested.

4). <u>Pay attention to the other person's nonverbal signals.</u> Listeners use a speaker's words to get the "objective" meaning of a message, but they rely on nonverbal cues for the emotional and interpersonal meanings of a message.

Your knowledge of body language, tone of voice, and other nonverbal cues can give deeper understanding of what others are communicating.

Remember that these cues are available not only when the other person is speaking but also when you are talking. If you often get signals that your listener is drifting away, you might be going overboard on irrelevant details or, perhaps, hogging the conversation. The antidote is active listening.

The key to effective listening is to devote active effort to the task. Although you won't experience a dramatic change in your speaking skills overnight, you can probably improve your listening abilities fairly quickly. Most people are ineffective listeners because they are unaware of the elements of effective listening-information you now possess. Also, effective listening hinges largely on your attitude. If you're willing to work at it, you can become a good listener.

Barriers to Effective Communication

The first one is "Defensiveness." Perhaps the most basic barrier to effective communication is defensiveness – an excessive concern with protecting oneself from being hurt. People usually react defensively when they feel threatened such as when they feel that others are going to evaluate them or when they believe that others are trying to control or manipulate them.

Defensiveness is also easily elicited when others act in a superior manner. Thus, those who flaunt their status, wealth, brilliance, or power often put receivers on the defensive.

Dogmatic people who convey "I'm always right" also tend to breed defensiveness in others; you need to remember that you don't have complete control over other's perceptions and reactions.

A threat need not be real to elicit defensive behavior. Thus, if you persuade yourself that Brandon won't like you, your interactions with him will probably not be very positive. And id the self-fulfilling prophecy kicks in, you may produce the negative reaction your fear.

The second one is "Motivational Distortion." That is people can hear what they want to hear instead of what is actually being said.

Each person had a unique frame of reference-certain attitudes, values, and expectations-that can influence what he or she hears. Information that contradicts an individual's own views often produces emotional discomfort. One way to avoid such unpleasant feelings is to engage in selective attention, or actively choosing to attend to information that supports one's beliefs and ignoring information that contradict them.

Similarly, an individual may read meanings that are not intended into statements or jump to erroneous conclusions. This tendency to distort information occurs most often when people are discussing issues they feel strongly about. Certain topics (politics, racism, sexism, homosexuality, abortion) are often highly charged for both the sender and receiver. Misperceptions and miscommunication are especially likely to occur in these situations.

The third is "self-preoccupation." Who hasn't experienced the frustration of trying to communicate with someone who is so self-focused as to make enjoyable two-way conversation impossible? These people seem to talk to hear themselves talk. If you try to slip in a word about your problems, they cut you off by saying, "That's nothing. Listen what happened to me!" Further, self-preoccupied people rarely listen attentively. When another person is talking, they're wrapped up in rehearsing what they're going to say next. Because they are self-focused, these individuals are usually unaware of their negative impact on others.

Self-preoccupied people arouse negative reactions on others for several reasons. First, their remarks are usually so self-serving (seeking to impress, to gain unwarranted sympathy, and so on) that others find it offensive. Another problem is that they consistently take up more than their fair share of conversation time. Some individuals do both-talking only about themselves and doing so at great length. After a "conversation" with someone like this, listeners feel that they have been ignored. No wonder people try to avoid such individuals if they can.

If they can't, they usually respond only minimally to try to end the conversation quickly. Needless to say, people risk alienating others if they ignore the norm that conversations should involve a mutual sharing of information.

The next one is "Game Playing". I deal with this in another chapter entitled, "so you want to play games".

The final one is "Collusion'. In contrast to the other barriers to effective communication, collusion requires at least two willing partners-usually involved in an intimate relationship. In collusion, two people have an unspoken agreement to deny some problematic aspect off reality in order to sustain their relationship. To achieve this mutual denial, both suppress all discussion of the problem are. The classic example of collusion is the alcoholic partnership. Here, the alcoholic requires the partner to join him or her in denying the existence of a drinking problem. To maintain the relationship, the two people go to great lengths to avoid any comments about alcohol- related difficulties.

Over time, the drinking usually gets worse and the relationship often deteriorates, thereby making it more difficult for the partner to continue the collusion. Because it is based on a mutual agreement to deny a specific aspect of reality, collusion obviously thwarts effective communication.

Body Language

Body contact doesn't always involve sex. You can communicate with your body parts: head, the trunk, hands, legs and feet.

Frequently touching or scratching suggests nervousness (Harrigan et al., 1991).

When people lean toward you, it means they are interested in what you have to say. People use hand gestures while talking to emphasize what they are conveying.

This type of nonverbal communication conveys emotions. Positive feelings include standing or sitting close to those you care for or them often, and looking at them frequently.

The duration of eye contact is what is meaningful (Kleinke, 1986). I must also note that nonverbal communication is culture bound. The following is taken from the book, "Psychology Applied to Modern Life". "Like language, nonverbal signals are different in different cultures (Matsumoto, 1996). For instance, people of Northern European heritage tend to engage in less physical contact and keep a greater distance between themselves than people of Latin or Middle Eastern heritage. The United States is usually characterized as a medium-contact culture, but there is a lot of variability among ethnic groups. Sometimes cultural differences can be quite dramatic. For example, in Tibet, people greet their friends by sticking out their tongues (Ekman 1975)".

As I said before, body language doesn't always involved sex. Your bodies can connect because as I said before, women sometimes want to be held. Sometimes they want their bodies caress: the feet, thighs, breast, face, or just holding of the hands. All of which is a form of communication.

Put a love song on and dance closely with her, just holding her body close to yours. Then let her lay on your chest as the two of you move together. This is the best relationship to be in. I know that this is the kind that will last.

The Personal

Baby girl it's not all just about you. I like body contact also. I work out and I have a nice physique. I like when a women just start caressing my chest and shoulders. I like it when she softly touches my face.

Body Language

This comes with time. Let's say the situation when the woman was caught talking to another man. The guy didn't ask her what she was talking to him for, but is body language sometimes tells you different.

His body language may want to ask you, but he doesn't. You have to be able to pick this up. Then communicate with him, telling him what the two of you were discussing. You can simply ask him what do he thinks about this, (the conversation you had). You are putting him in the mix and at the same time letting him know what the conversation was about.

She comes home hurting. If she doesn't say anything/ you should be able to detect that something is wrong with her. The same applies to the woman. Women have the habit of immediately thinking they did something wrong. So they will follow you around until they get a positive response.

This is true communication and the kind that causes the relationship to last. There is nothing wrong with blowing kisses at each other. It signals to the other that you are still interested in them. Effective communication is vital to a lasting marriage (Cleek & Pearson, 1985).

More Nonverbal Communication

Communication isn't all about words. As a matter of fact I believe that 80% of what someone says isn't coming from the mouth, but other nonverbal cues.

According to (Stewart, Cooper, Stewart & Friedley, 1998) females are better readers of nonverbal cues than men.

I find this to be true myself dealing with my first love. Almost every morning and sometimes in the afternoon, she would pay close attention to me. The way I move or look at her would be the way she knew if I wanted to be bothered.

If she picked up cues (nonverbal) that I didn't want to be bothered. She would stay away from me and watch me from a distance. My point is even though people aren't aware of it; nonverbal communication plays a vital role in life every day. People use nonverbal cues to convey their true feelings to others. If you dislike someone, people usually convey their feelings through nonverbal channels.

Personal Space

Personal space is said to be a circle where you want to be only yours. Individuals you like or admire, the more comfortable you feel standing or being physically close to them. There are exceptions, such as parties, or any crowded area. Women sit or stand closer together then men do when talking.

If someone stands too close to you that you aren't close to or comfortable with. You will stand back or back up. The message (nonverbal cue) you are sending to them is to stand your distance. We aren't cool like that.

Facial Expression

More than anything else, face expressions convey emotions. I remember one time when my girl was upset when I gave someone else more attention than her. She came around several times to see if I was going to acknowledge her. I did in a way, but it wasn't to her standard. So she would get by herself and look sad. My dude noticed it and said that something was on her mind seriously. I knew the problem, so I went and paid her the attention she wanted. She was cool after that. My girl could look at my face expression and read what was on my mind.

Eye Contact

Eye contact (also called mutual gaze) is another way to convey emotions. It's just not the eye contact but the duration of the eye contact that means something. Eye contact conveys interest and respect. Couples in live spend a lot of time gazing at each other (Patterson, 1988).

My girl and I always did this-even after we broke up. It didn't matter what we did or what we would be doing. We would always look at the other to see what they were doing. The message we were sending was yes I'm doing what I'm doing but my mind is on you.

Detecting Deception

How many times your mate told you that they aren't upset, but their tone of voice conveyed something totally different? You could see it in their body movement that they were really upset.

Most liars leak cues from a nonverbal cues.

Visual Cues

- Excessive blinking
- Dilation of the pupils
- Nervously touch themselves more than normal

Vocal Cues

- Speaking with a higher pitch
- Giving relatively short answers
- Excessive hesitations and stammering

CHAPTER 5 The Best Relationship to be in (Part 2)

(Keys that Unlock the Road to a Lasting Intimate Relationship)

Now I will begin with Trust.

When you trust someone, you have a firm belief or confidence in the honesty, integrity, reliability, justice, etc., of another person.

I love this trust thing. It grows too. I have had several males and females tell me that it's hard for them to trust again. What they are really saying is that they are not going to fall in love easily or quickly again.

Trust vs. Love

Trust leads to love. When individuals say it's hard for me to trust. What they are saying is that it's hard for them to fall in love again.

Philip R. Shaver of the University of California described them as, "avoidant adults". These individuals both fear and feel uncomfortable about getting close to others. They are reluctant to trust others and prefer to maintain emotional distance from others. They have the lowest incidence of positive relationship experiences of the three groups. Avoidant adult do and see their mothers as cold and rejecting."

My take on this is I believe that in the beginning of the relationship you don't fall in love, but you can trust. Love isn't trust, vice versa.

Attributes of Trust

Cooking

The two of you have just started dating and already I'm cooking for you. You don't love me, but you trust that I put something in your food. You eat my food. You trust me.

Exchanging Information

You don't love me, but you gave me your home address and number. I can say you trust me. I may be a murderer or a rapist from another state.

When I called you and told you to get ready because I am coming to pick you up. You get ready and waited for me. This is trust. You trust me to do what I said I would do.

Let's Get Deeper

Complete trust is what makes the relationship last. When you see your girl talking to another man, you don't ask her what they were talking about. You trust that is was professional.

The wife comes into play in this situation. This is where the communication with the body language comes into play. If you see that it bothers him a little, just tell him voluntarily what the two of you were talking about. We are still human beings.

I told you it's about the both of you and not one of you. So knowing that he won't ask you about it, you should do this freely having nothing to hide.

The Rumor

Remember the situation about the woman who suffered mentally because of the rumor put out on her on her job?

Well, the man in this situation plays a vital role. What you don't want to do is accuse or question her about it. Completely trusting her means you go to her, understanding that she is hurting and say to her sincerely. Look baby, I love you so much, I know you would never sleep with another man. You are my queen. You honor your body and your man. You would never do anything to hurt me baby. I know this and will die behind that belief.

Then you begin to passionately kiss her. Then just tell her how beautiful she is. Sit back and watch her cry. The only thing that matters to her is my response. I just told her last night that I love and trust her, but my actions, acting off my emotions showed different. I don't understand the fact that I accused her farther destroyed her mentally. Her tears now are them of pain.

You are supposed to be supportive of her. This would draw the two of you closer together. You have healed her and you comforted her. This is the kind of relationship you want to be in.

Now there is the case when you know the woman you are dealing with cheats. You just can't catch her. That's another subject.

The Man's Test

Remember I spoke about the man who is working around a woman who only wants to seduce him? Well, in this situation, the woman must counter attack this. First, she has to do something to help him get the woman off of his mind. I believe, when she puts it on him. He won't be thinking about another woman. Then you sex him until he doesn't have any energy left

to have sex with another woman. You have to meet his needs. Then when you finish, walk around in something seductive. You watched when he is standing at attention-put it on him again. My suggestion is you go get on top of him and do you, looking him eye to eye-taking the pain letting him knows that you have all he need at home. Then send him to work with you on his mind letting him know that you trust him. You want it to work. You have to make it work. Your man needs you. So you better be there for him.

4. Commitment

"According to Robert Sternberg's (1986, 1988). Commitment involves the decision and intent to maintain a relationship in spite of the difficulties and costs that may arise. According to Sternberg, commitment has a short-term and long-term aspect. The short-term aspect concerns the conscious decision to love someone. The long-term aspect reflects the determination to make a relationship endure." Remember that man who refused to hold that woman? Well commitment is holding that woman when she wants to be held. You must do this with a smile on your face even if you don't like to do so. Learn to like it because to make it work you have to adapt it if you want the relationship to last in peace.

5. Sacrifice

When you sacrifice for someone you give up something special to you to benefit them. Sacrifice is not true sacrifice under pressure. It has to be a willing sacrifice. This is the true one that causes the relationship to last.

I dealt, remember, with the woman who had the gambling problem? Her home and marriage was on the line. In spite of all of this she still refused to stop going to the casino. The man gave all but she didn't. The truth of the matter was that they were giving up the extra money for the better of both of them. Complete sacrifice would have meant the two of you still together and all of your bills paid. If the man decided to walk away from the relationship, it was the woman's choice that caused it.

Complete sacrifice must be exercised by the both of you. Sacrifice may mean giving up something you love to do to make it last. It may be something as simple as too much time with your friends and not your girl or it may be pervert sex acts that's understood to destroy relationships in the process of time. It's bad to put friends before your mate. She is supposed to be first place after God. Your friends are supposed to be the ones complaining about you not

spending time with them and never your girl. This is true and complete sacrifice. I believe this kind will last, because it is done in love. There is nothing wrong with hanging with your friends. Something is only wrong with it when your girl isn't receiving the quality time she deserves. The man is supposed to want to do this. This is the attitude he is supposed to have when it comes to his girl. His attitude supposed to be if she's not happy. Then I'm not happy. So in this attitude I will stop whatever I am doing to see about my love and I won't leave until she is showing me that pretty smile.

In the beginning of the relationship, you have to start off doing this. This is what you have done in the beginning anyway before you scored. Didn't it work? Well shy stop now?

Before the two of you ever meet, you both had a schedule that you followed. Now that you have someone you feel special in your life. You will want to rearrange that schedule making sure that they are a part of it.

6. Submission

Wives are commanded to submit yourself to your husband, as you are doing it to the Lord (Ephesians 5:22). The Greek word for submit is "hupotass" and it means to subordinate: relax, to obey-be under obedience.

The position of the woman is t to recognize the headship of her husband (v.230, be subject to him (v.24), and reverence him (v.33). But he must respect her also.

True and complete submission must be done by the wife. This submission is to never become a degrading one.

Degrading Submission

Never submit to someone telling you to sell your body or drugs. This isn't pure submission. This is stupidly and foolishness. I mean why would you allow your girl to be sexed by another man? A misunderstanding of true and pure Godly submission could be bad. I believe at times submissive individuals often allow people to take advantage of them. These people have a problem with saying no to unreasonable requests. They have a problem voicing their disagreement in a situation that may arise.

Social approval to others could be the motive behind this conduct. Whatever the case, it leads to resentful of the individual who is taking advantage.

This often provokes the submissive person to try to punish the other person by withdrawing, sulking, or crying (Bower & Bower, 1991).

When a man does this, it simply means he doesn't truly love that woman. Because if he did, he would never put her in any position to degrade herself all he does toward her would be for her good. It's never to destroy her mentally, physically, or spiritually.

So wives you submit to your mate when he is obeying God because it's to better you which in return better the relationship.

Remember the two situations I spoke about when the woman warns the man about the other woman who was constantly trying to get him to yield to her by constantly touching and bumping into him?

Women can because of the female brain—they have the ability to quickly assess the thoughts, intentions, and beliefs of others. This comes from the smallest hints. This is how they know things about people around them. Their gut feelings are actual physical sensations that translate messages to certain areas in their brain.

Just think about the times in life when your girl told you not to go a certain place or hang with a certain person. We took this to mean that they were trying to keep us home just to be with them, when indeed they were trying to save us. Most of the time when we refuse to listen, we end up getting in some kind of trouble.

So in the situation above she is not to submit to you and allow you to disrespect her with that other woman. That's a form of affection.

Your wife told you not to allow that other woman to touch on you or wrestle with you. Some women say they can handle it but the truth is handling it isn't the problem. You are in a relationship that you are supposed to live by principles. This is if you desire it to last.

Now I understand if you are in the relationship just for the ride and do not anticipate it lasting. Then that is another story but if you desire to make it last. Then the principle is respect which I will deal with later.

Respect means I don't disrespect her behind her back.

This isn't about you being able to prevent sexual contact. It's about you not even wanting another man to touch on your body or another woman. You being a woman should never permit this kind of behavior. That is one of the reason you have a man. This is what I meant in chapter one when I said your mate is to be your main focus. You don't just cleave to them for sex. If you want to touch on another woman, go home and do it. If you want to wrestle, call your girl and tell her baby let's get it on. If you don't like to play like that, then you better get with the program before it becomes a heart condition.

It would hurt me if I ever catch my girl touching or wrestling with another man. I would tell her about it, letting her know that I can't handle it. If she continues to do this, I have to walk away before she is constantly hurting me on purpose. I will not be in an up and down or unfaithful relationship.

If she tries to argue about it, telling me that there isn't anything going on between them. Then it's more to it. She may secretly be attracted to him. You mean to tell me that I gave up my porn and my being a playboy to make it work. You have the audacity to argue with me so you could continue to wrestle with another man. I'll tell you what. You and your heart ache get out my house and life and go be with him. If it doesn't work with you, then someone else must be God's plan for me-bye.

In any situation when you are in a relationship, to let an outsider touch on your body in just about any kind of way will end in sorrow if you don't stop this behavior.

CHAPTER 6 THE Best relationship to be in (part 3)
(Keys that unlock the road to a lasting intimate relationship)

When you refuse to give this behavior up, you are actually saying that you don't want the relationship to work.

NBA Potential

Take the guy who had the great basketball potential. He refused to listen to his girl's advice telling him to get a job and stop selling drugs.

He could have stopped selling drugs, got a job while going to school until he received his big breaks. You may not make the money you did selling drugs, but at least you stayed free. You could stay with your girl and raise your child.

In 7 ½ years you could have been the first round pick or a pick in the NBA draft. Then you could have set your family straight financially for life.

In this chapter, I will deal with respect and two different kinds of love. One is conditional and the other is unconditional.

7. Respect

A man who respects his mate never, I mean he never puts his hands on her vice versa. If he has to beat on her then he doesn't need her. I hate when a man hits on a woman or a woman who beats her husband up. Because when you hurt them mentally, physically or spiritually, it's a sign that you have falling out of love with them. It's proof that you don't have respect for them.

If you loved them, hurting them would be hurting yourself. This will break you down to end your pain if indeed you have participated in such actions. If you respect them you would feel and show honor and esteem for them. You would hold them in high regard. You wouldn't intrude on their dignity. When you put your hands on them you begin destroying them mentally forcing them to live with you in fear. Never do this.

Abusive Relationships

Abuse could take place by you calling her out of her name or telling her that she will never be nothing in life or she isn't nothing. It could be you neglecting her because women hate to be ignored. It goes against their makeup which is to be liked and socially connected. They are designed to crave attention. It's your job to give it to them.

You could abuse them sexually by being extreme in the bed and force them to do things they are very much against. Women stay in abusive relationships because they dread economic hardship and believe they won't be able to make it on their own (Choice & Lamke, 1997). Women fear being without a home (Browne, 1993). Others are afraid to face disapproval from loved ones. Because may be a loved one knew something wasn't right but they hide it (Barnett & La Violette, 1993). Some fear being hurt further or getting killed (DeMaris & Swinford, 1996)

She is your mate. You are supposed to be one with her. Women you don't need to go through hell to try to be happy. I believe you could be in a relationship and never be made to cry unless it's because of passionate sex. I believe both parties can remain faithful until death do them part. I believe the sex can remain great in the beginning all the way until the grave.

I know we are human and make mistakes; but do we have to? Why do I have to make a mistake out of anger and call my girl out of her name? When I could calm down then approach my girl, for this reason I believe that we could be put into situations that we handle rightly. Whereby we never have to say we are sorry.

I just believe these things could happen.

Total respect means that you never kiss another man or woman while in a relationship with someone. You never touch on their bodies in an appropriate way or allow them to do you the same, not even in a playing manner. I don't care how strong the desire gets.

Total respect means never disrespecting them. It means you never pay attention to porn. You have a wife or husband at home. Go home and ask them to get naked for you and watch them.

You say you are tired of her. Then fall back in love with her. Get you attention off that other woman and put it back on your girl. I told you to let her seat of love (breast) satisfy you at all times. This isn't done some of the times. Not just 5 or 10 years but until death do you part. Let her love enrapture you always continue to give her your attention and total affection. I deal with the power of affection in another chapter.

Total respect means respecting you. I know, whenever you allow a man to call you out of your name. That is disrespect. It's even worse if you like it and begin to call yourself that name. Because with that name comes a spirit which will produce a behavior. It's disrespect to allow a man to put his hands on you to hurt you.

You don't respect your body when you put drugs or alcohol in it. You are literally destroying yourself.

8. Love

This is twofold. It's the love between the woman and the man. This love is Eros and God's love – which is agape. One is conditional and the other is unconditional.

Eros is a sexual love or desire. It's a God given desire that must be operated in the environment of self-control.

A woman who has a man to dedicate to her, trust her, communicate with her, commit to her, listen to her Godly instinct, sacrifices for her, and respects her. She falls in Eros with him. The only way this doesn't evolve into love is if one of the two is acting liking children playing games.

When you fall in love with someone you become one with them. Their pain and happiness becomes yours. I don't believe everything I hear. Especially when majority believes in it one thing I don't believe is that old saying that love hurts or pain. Love is too beautiful.

Now what I do believe is that a heart could be broken that's in love. If that is the pain people are talking about then I'm not with that.

You only experience pain when one of the individuals fallout of love. You're only hurt when this begins to happen or the individual acts off of uncontrolled anger and does something to hurt those they love because they hurt them. True love won't continue to hurt those it loves. In the love atmosphere, the woman or the man never has to worry about the other sleeping around on them. When you love someone you won't touch another man or a woman sexually.

Here is why.

You understand that this will crush your spouse. So in turn it will affect you. This is when two become one. This is what makes the relationship so beautiful.

Love Breeds Security

I love an independent woman. I like when she has an attitude to survive with or without a man. This is one of the most beautiful women to me. It attracts me because she will get hers. She doesn't sit at home and cry about what she can't do or what people don't want to give her or do for her. She gets off of her back and work for hers.

Love breeds security. Women like that I would that her and one of my goals will be to make everything ease for her. Her work ethic attracts me. If she been hurt, I will help remove those scares with compassionate love. Whatever she desires and lack I will make sure she gets it

What a lot of individuals fail to understand is that love doesn't take from. Love gives. When you love or want to love someone. You are all about their well-being. You change for them to better the relationship. You will make sure they are secure if something was to happen to you.

When a man tries to hold a woman or use tactics to keep them there beside them. This isn't true love. Passion may be there because of the sex. But love sets her free to live. It puts her in a position to leave whenever she wants to.

If she is crazy enough to leave, then let her. She anticipated that anyway.

Love breeds Protection

When you love someone you protect them from anything that would harm them. Being unfaithful harms them emotionally. So why do you do it? It's simple. You don't love her.

If another man puts his hands on your wife, you are supposed to put him on his back. Protect her life with your very own.

In your love, you shield her from physical, spiritual, and mental abuse.

Spiritual Protection

In your love for her, you would guide her in the ways of God. Because you understand that this will set her up good for eternity with God.

This protection requires keeping deception from her spirit. You will help to build her spirit man up by surrounding with spiritual things. This goes for the woman also.

Physical Protection

I spoke on this already. It's worth doing so again because of its prevalence. This means in your love for her. You physical protect her from being hurt by you or anyone else. This is your job.

This also means you instruct her on ways to preserve her body. You will make sure the home is secure when she lies down to sleep or rest.

Mental Protection

Love protects their mate's minds from anything that would hurt them mentally. This means verbal abuse or anything that will destroy them mentally. Mental protection means you say nothing or do nothing that destroys their mind set.

The following on love is taken from "Psychology Applied to Modern Life".

Gender Difference Regarding Love

The stereotype holds that women are more romantic than men. Nonetheless, much of the research evidence suggests just the opposite-that men are the more romantic gender (Dion & Dion, 1988). For example, men hold more romantic beliefs. (Love lasts forever "or" There is one perfect love in the world for everyone") (Peplau, Hill, & Rubin, 1993).

In addition men fall in love more easily than women, whereas women fall out of love more easily than men (Hill, Rubin, & Peplau, 1976; Rubin, Peplau, & Hill, 1981).

Women are more likely to report physical symptoms associated with being in love. Such as feeling like they are "Floating on a cloud" (Peplau & Gordon, 1985), and they are somewhat more likely to verbalize and display tender emotions (Dindia & Allen, 1992).

"Women show they are in love in their memory circuits, gut feelings, and the attention they give the person" That is not taken from the college book.

According to Cindy Hazan and Phillip Shaver (1987), adult romantic love and infant attachment share a number of features: intense fascinations with the other person, distress at separation, and efforts to stay close and spend time together.

According to Robert Sternberg's (1986, 1988), triangular theory of love posits that all

Love experiences are made up of three components: intimacy, passion, and commitment.

Intimacy

Intimacy refers to warmth, closeness, and sharing in a relationship. Signs of intimacy include giving and receiving emotional support, valuing the loved one, wanting to promote the welfare of the loved one and sharing one's self and one's possession with another.

Self-disclosure is necessary to achieve and maintain feelings of intimacy in a relationship whether platonic or romantic.

Passion

Passion refers to the intense feelings (both positive and negative) experienced in love relationships, including sexual desire. Passion is related to drives that lead to romance, physical attraction, and sexual consummation. Although sexual needs may be dominant in many close relationships, other needs also figure in the experience of passion, including the needs for nurturance, self-esteem, dominance, submission, and self-actualization. For example, self-esteem is threatened when one experiences jealousy.

Passion obviously figures most prominently in romantic relationships. The third one is commitment. I dealt with this already in another chapter. I will now give you my theory.

Love vs. Passion

There is a difference between love and passion. Many couples today still believe they are in love while at the same time cheating. In actuality, they have a passion for each other.

Passion without love hurts. Love isn't passion but they go hand and hand. I can have a passion to destroy you and everything about you. But if I love you I won't do anything to hurt you.

Unconditional Love

This kind of love loves without strings and conditions. It's a supernatural love. God can only give you this.

It's a love that loves the unlovable and the undesirable. This love you must have in your relationship also. It overrides and over looks everything and loves the individual in spite.

This is the agape love. This is the love that shows affection and gives benevolence. It loves in a social and moral sense.

In the book of first Corinthians Paul gives us a clear example of it in chapter 13. He said that this kind of love is patience. It suffers long, believes the best about a person because it has hope. It endures all things that comes its way and still loves (v 4, 7).

This love is very generous, not jealous or envious (v 4). Its attribute is to be courtesy. This means it doesn't act unseemly, but it's always polite to everyone. It's not rude or discourteous (v 5). It's very unselfish. Never sour, bitter, seeks only the good of others. Its attribute is not to seek revenge by retaliating (v 5). It controls itself and is never resentful (v 5). It hates when people are wronged. It is never quick to expose the wrong of people. This is because it believes the best out of people in spite of what they did (v 6, 7).

This love has a sincere motive in its conduct. It's not conceited or boastful, always honest, leaves no impression because it deals with what is strictly true. It knows how to be silent and trust. It's joyful and truthful.

It's poured out in you when you make Jesus Christ the Lord of your life (Roman 5:5, 10:9, 10). It grows as you obey God's word (1John

2:5) and practice it on other (3:18). This love ministers about no effects of injurious to his near (Roman 13:10).

Now you tell me what's wrong with including this kind of love in your intimate relationship. There are no bad attributes. Everything is good about it.

You want the relationship to truly last until death due you part. Then add this powerful love to your relationship. You won't be sorry. I put my life on it.

Part Four

When the game is played you either win or lose.

It's funny when you play the game and always end up on the losing end. Now you're left with regret, pain, and sorrow. Remember though, it was your own choice to play.

© 2014 by Glenn C. Damond

CHAPTER 1 So You Want to Play Games

Game playing was first described by psychologist Eric Berne (1964). In this project, games are manipulative interactions with predictable outcomes, in which people conceal their real motives.

The apostle Paul had something to say about game playing. He recorded, "when I was a child, I spoke as a child, I understood as a child I thought as a child: but when I became a man, I put away childish things." (1 Corinthians 13:11).

Paul meant that in his life when he became an adult. He didn't respond to life's situations and circumstances as a child would.

Let's get deeper.

The Greek word for put away is "katargeo" and it means to make useless or void; abolish; leave unemployed. It farther means that the things (childish ways in which you respond to life) that cease are to be superseded by a more complete life along the same lines, in the same way that adulthood is so far advanced beyond childhood as to be on another plane entirely (Finis Jennings Dake, 2001).

I say that games are immature tactics in which insecure individuals propagate. In that they inaugurate the beginning of a couple dying off in their intimate relationship (Glenn C. Damond, 2014).

When people play games they are saying that they don't want the relationship at hand to work. When you play games you create a time bomb in someone that could go off. What you are doing is you are literally forcing the one you said you love to begin to have bad feelings toward you.

Then you have the audacity to sit back and wonder why the two of you are not getting along. Why the two of you are on the verge of a separation.

Children play games. When you do so you are in a childlike state. You profess you love him or her, but if you really did. You would be moved to make them smile when they are upset. I wouldn't sit right with you to know that your loved one is in a bad move.

But you are the one who is causing this. Then you know what you are doing, and you still want to play with their hearts.

You sit back and push buttons to feel in control or some kind of power with your immature self.

Today we exchange trust for this destructive force. Women in particular have the ability to know if someone loves them because the female brain is geared to tracking moment by moment, the nonverbal signals of the innermost feelings of others. But you still want to play games instead of trusting me.

A friend of mines named Mark was put into a situation by his girlfriend that caused him his freedom, 15 years of it. She wanted to see if he could protect her. So she created a situation whereby another man approached her while he was with her. Mark felt disrespected so he reacted. It turned out bad for him, but the dude she used couldn't even protect her. He was the cause of Mark going to prison.

Females, instead of sitting down talking to their man and learning of him-may be even becoming longtime friends. They create situations to see what kind of dude they have. They create situations to see if he is the jealous type, seeing how he reacts when she's around other men. I'm not promoting jealousy because I believe women are more jealous type. Is that a reason for you not to fall in love with him? I don't think so. You're not perfect. Which means you will have something about you. That he doesn't like.

What am I saying is this? If you know that it makes him upset when you do certain things with other men. Why do it? Here is where the game playing comes in at. Let's say we have a disagreement about something small. It may be over what color the house is or what school the children will attend.

Say the woman doesn't get her way. She will most likely react off emotions. She may be driven to do something to make her mate upset, something she knows that makes him upset. This is just because she didn't get her way.

She sits back and watches his reactions and inside says to herself "you should have wanted what I wanted." Her hidden agenda is to make him upset because she is upset over something so small.

"Particularly problematic are repetitive games that result in bad feelings and erode the trust and respect that are essential to good relationships. Games interfere with effective communication and are a destructive element in relationships. (Taken from Psychology Applied to Modern Life."

Games caused trouble in relationship. They affect not only communication but the consummation of the relationship. This is the overall picture. This is why you have to put away childish ways. You have to make them useless and void.

This person is like this because of the environment they were brought up in. They were taught to play mind games with their mate.

Another Example of Game Playing

Females have the tendency to act out when they can't get a certain man's attention. They may like the guy and does so many things to try to get his attention, but doesn't. Instead of just going to him and telling him how she feels. She waits and waits, playing little mind games to get her point across. My first soul tie did this a lot.

Example One

She may pretend she likes another guy that's close to him just to see how he responds to that. Her hidden agenda is to see if he will get upset at her interest in another man. This is rejection to the guy. People are usually turned off by others who reject them (Wright & Contrada, 1986).

Reciprocal Liking

An old adage advises, "If you want to have a friend, be a friend." This suggestion captures the idea of the reciprocity principle in relationships. Reciprocal liking refers to liking those who show that they like you.

Many studies have demonstrated that if you believe another person likes you. You will like him or her in return (Berscheid & Walster, 1978; Kenny, 1994).

My point is to let you know to grow up and be the gentlemen and lady our world needs. Stop adding to the statistics of the couples breaking up, instead increase those who are the one's that's truly lasting until death do the two of you part.

Change Starts in the Mind

People can say I will be a better person or I will try to be a better person. I'm sure we have all said this time and time again. But have you ever realized that you are in the same position you were years ago.

This is because change starts in the mind (Romans 12:2). When you change the way you think. You change the way you govern your life (Proverbs 23:7).

Now to a stubborn person this is like a brick wall. Because everybody wants to believe that their way of thinking is the best and right way of thinking. Let's think about this for a moment. What has my way of thinking did for me that benefit me until the point of have rue peace within myself while doing it.

I mean I was taught as a woman if a man cheats on me. I return him the favor. What I have done is exposed myself to another man. It might have been someone I don't even know- remember women operate mostly off emotions. Or it may be someone I secretly wanted to give myself to.

Now I'm feeling upset inside. I came down off my emotional ride. Now I feel ashamed because now the relationship between the guy and I gave myself has went to another level.

But this is what you were taught to do. When in actuality if he cheats on you, then he fell out of love with you. Because if he truly was in love with you. It would hurt him to lay with another woman.

This is a relationship you don't want to be into because it leads to trouble and scares. These scares can be carried over to your next mate and cause that relationship to be destroyed.

You have to recognize when a man isn't in love with you. You sitting there try to figure out what you're not doing right, when in fact he has his focus on another woman.

He is not playing his role. This is why the relationship isn't working. You could stay in that relationship because people change. But if I were you, I wouldn't allow someone to hurt me purposely.

Sex

I won't go into detail here because I will deal with this subject in another chapter. But I will say this. God originally ordained sex to be enjoyed in the marriage relationship between the woman and the man.

Now if the sexual activities I'm indulging in is leading me to desire someone else in the bedroom with me and my girl. Then I must be participating in something that's forbidden by God

We only have to use common sense. I mean common if the life style I'm living is causing me trouble. Then change that lifestyle.

Game Playing

Let's say that my wife and I go to the ball game with some friends. Now before we left the house we had a disagreement and things didn't go her way. Now she is her childish zone begin to ask our friends about her old boyfriend because she knows this makes me upset. If I allow her to see that she is getting to me, she wins.

Now as a man intentionally putting me in a position to resent her and plan on getting her back. Now I feel like this because the woman who told me she loved me is causing me to do this. I didn't say I was going to act off my emotions. I'm just showing you how game playing is destructive.

I'm a man of integrity. So I will do the right thing. I'll sit her down and explain her immature actions and make her realized how it affects me. If she continues to do things to make me upset, then I will take it to say that she's not interested in making the relationship work.

Game playing is a serious issue. This is why Paul says to leave the childish ways unemployed. When you are at this level, game playing won't have a chance to go to working on destroying the relationship.

"In the broadest sense, game playing can include the deliberate (or sometimes unintentional) use of ambiguous, indirect, or deceptive statements. Some game playing involves "verbal fencing" to avoid having to make clear one's meaning or intent. (Taken from Psychology Applied to Modern Life)."

Moreover, game playing shouldn't be exercised in any relationship.

In conclusion, if a man isn't a gentleman and woman isn't a lady, this will destroy the relationship ultimately. This is because the gentlemen know his position in society and the lady knows her role. Together they last until death due the two of us part.

CHAPTER 2 When to Play the Game (if ever)

In previous chapter, I spoke against game playing, but in this chapter I'll reveal to you when to play the game.

We have to always understand that we are dealing with human beings-not all are spiritually connected. So they are almost all of the time react according to their nature.

Its human nature to take things for granted we are governed by that nature that doesn't appreciate something or someone that's of value of you. It is only when that special person is taking away from us that we then begin to appreciate them.

Psychologist Theodor Reik, we only learn to love only through rejection. This is something embedded in us as long as we live. When we go through some kind of rejection, we then turn the tables to be the chaser of that love we once rejected.

Suffering has a way to get our attention and motivate us to end of suffering by doing what is only right for us to do.

Think about it! More time is spent in a day talking and thinking about someone that dies. Your mind begins to reminisce about old times. You may have been the last person they talked to or seen.

You begin to think about how their death could have been avoided and on and on. Your appreciation for them grows. This is in their absence.

Let's take it to the relationship level.

The Cry of the Bruised Heart

I was in some relationships like this .With Tee, I use to make her jealous (when she played games) by entertaining other females. She couldn't handle it. She would stare at me while I was doing it, and then afterward pick a fight with me. When she tried to make me jealous I would turn my head on her. I kept her wondering if I wanted her anymore or was I losing interest.

When I gave my attention and showed off my body to other women on purpose. This killed her. She would then do things to get my attention back. Something she knew I liked. She would think I'm mad at her when I don't look at her. So this rejection would make her follow me around and stay up under me or just watch me majority of the day. This is because rejection hurts like physical pain in both males and females- especially from a loved one.

All the while I was playing the game she was. It was almost like I only could get some attention from her when I seem like I'm not interested in her. She would begin to be obsessed with me, watching me for hours without saying anything.

I hated doing her this but I know rejection or pain gets our attention as human. I also know because she is immature and not spiritually connected I was in for a ride. I also know and understand something about human nature.

The Challenged Nature

People, especially women love a challenge. I fell in my first soul ties' hands even though our relationship started as an affair. I found out about the other guy she was involved with. I attempted to back up. She told me not to because anything could happen. She was doing what women are designed to do which is to keep their options open. I continued to pursue by writing her and caused her to fall for me without never having touched her physically but I touched her mentally in ways a man had never done.

It had gotten to the point where she could actually feel when I'm hurting and know what I am thinking without me even saying a word. She would immediately do something or say something to make me feel alright. It was only so much she could do.

We stop messing around about 3 times and end up messing back around. She told me twice she didn't want to mess around. I told her 3 times. It was like when she told me I wanted her even more. I got obsessed with her. It was the same when I told her until this day she is obsessed with me now because all I do is play mind games with her.

I make her chase me now while a lot of other men or chasing her. The relationship is this way because she took me for granted. I gave her a good man and she started messing with my friend. I stoop to her level and started messing with other women. She wanted me more than ever. I fell in her lap. I was too good to be true. So instead of walking away for good, I played the game with her.

She chased me because I became a challenge to her. The law of scarcity states that when someone is told that they can't have something- according to psychologists (Brehm & Brehm, 1981; Williams et al., 1993). They often want what they can't have any more.

This is because people want what they can't have. When a person isn't spiritually connected they function from human behavior. If they are spiritually connected, they would function from the spiritual when their nature tries to dictate to them otherwise. This is doing unto others what they want done to them. (Matt 7:12).

When you overdo yourself with an immature person you actually begin to diminish your value. In their eyes you are theirs and you're not going anywhere. They know you are a good person but their human nature begin to take you for granted and mess with someone else.

This is because they feel they have you. People want what they can't have. According to (Ialdini, this belief originates from two sources. First we have learned as individuals that items that are hard to get must be of better quality them items that are easy to get. Hence, the principle of scarcity. Secondly as stated before, when people's choices are restricted in some way, rather it's a mate, job, or product. This only makes them want what they can't have even more.

According to (Brehm, 1966) the psychological term for this is reactance.

Yes they may have wanted a good person in their lives but their human nature says something different. Good people have standards they live by. Therefore, if you do want to keep that good person, you better change your ways to keep them. People can put up with so much. Then they are out of here.

So when to play games. It's when you are taking for granted. Threaten to leave them and watch how the tables turn. If they truly love you and want to keep you then they will get their minds right.

I don't strongly advice game playing. I do advice you to be with someone who doesn't play games at all. But if you must play the game because you really want this person and you understand that they are immature-and this is a tactic you use to get them right. So you could explain to them when they come to you the situation. Then do what you do.

The Spiritual Connection

This is why I believe that it isn't good to leave God out your relationship rather intimate or otherwise. God ordained intimate relations between a woman and a man (Genesis 2:18). So if he ordained them, don't you think he knows how to cause them to work?

Think about your life right now. You may be in a relationship where someone is cheating. You may be bruised mentally or physically. Do you really believe God designed that for you? Do you really think he ordained for relationships to function up and down-the two of you break up today or be back together next week?

I mean if he ordained something for you to enjoy. While are you suffering inwardly. If he created it, then it's good according to (James 1:17).

We run to every known source on the subject and then turn around and have the audacity to wonder why it isn't working. It's just like saying that you created an invention. Its common sense to have instructions for that invention whereby it could function properly.

You would be amazed at all of the pain you could miss if only you trust God's instructions in your intimate relationships. When a female plays games with you trying to hurt you in some way, you don't respond. A female told me when a woman play games with you; you don't play back with them. You just ignore them. Don't pay them any mind. This will hurt her more. This will drive her.

But she'll want you even more because this is what she wants a man who doesn't play games. This is the man she'll bend over backwards to keep. This means she'll whatever to keep you happy. She won't give up on you. This is when she finds that strong man after dealing with a lot of weak men. This is the man of integrity.

CHAPTER 3 The Natural and the Unnatural

People believe that life isn't made up any right and wrong as many would like us believe. To everything in life there is a natural function and unnatural. Common sense, which sometimes we forget to use-will tell us that if my natural function of a thing (sex, money, food, etc) produces bad results. Then my natural must in actuality to an unnatural.

Sex

We were created with common sense. If you are reading this book, then my guess is you believe in God. If you do, then you believe he ordain relationships to exist between women and men because he created them.

Now let's think about it. In my sex bed if I'm producing a negative result. It's just because I'm introducing activities within my sex bed that's not supposed to be there.

A negative result can mean I'm getting tired of my mate and I now want to get rid of my mate to enter new experiences with another mate. The natural way is one woman and a man.

Have you ever noticed that you get tired of that next mate? It goes on and on. Now women have 3 baby daddies. Just use common sense. Do you really think this is natural? Is it natural for you to go from one man to the next man, or one woman to the next? Is it natural?

I mean we are talking about a God who is perfect. So what he creates follows this pattern. If he indeed ordained for man and woman to be as one, then he must have the natural function to sustain that relationship.

I talk about them throughout this book. If you don't receive or believe them, then just take a look at your life. In my sex bed, why am I at a level whereby I have to sex more women than my mate. I have a mate at home. Then why do I give my attention to all of these other women. Why do I love to watch naked women when I could watch my wife?

Why do I participate in this action that always produces negative results? The answer is simple. You are functioning in an unnatural way. What you've been taught on how to govern your sex life is wrong. If you are brutish to still think it's an unnatural function; then why you want to be sexed by two men at the same time? Why you let more than 5 men sex you one after the other in one day? Men, why you have to have sex with 5 different women a day?

You are dying off in your sex life and don't even know it. In another chapter, I show you how to come out of that problem. Have you ever wondered why you can't find a good man or a good woman? Have you ever wondered why you are always alone: can't get peace or true happiness, forced to stay with a mate that you are not happy with. I mean why are you unhappy? Is it because you are not satisfied? But I thought you loved this person to death. In the beginning, you were crazy about them. You couldn't stop thinking about them. But why did that natural function stop?

It's natural because everything between the two of you was good. You talked about marriage, etc. But now you are on the verge of breaking up. What went wrong? You went wrong and refused to admit it. In actuality, your natural function is really an unnatural function.

It's natural when the good positive results stem from it. Come on people! We are using what God gave us-common sense.

Drugs

If it is natural for me to take drugs of any kind, then who do the always produce bad results? I'm stealing from my kids or family to support my habit. I find myself doing just about anything to get some drugs.

At the age of 13(as I said already) I started using drugs. It started with me puffing off of marijuana until the point when my body was addicted to it. I had to have it every day. I convinced myself to believe that it helps me talk right and say the right words to get in females paints.

I moved to cocaine. I snorted so much of it at 14 years old that I almost overdosed and killed myself. But we say this grows from the earth. So it's good. It's good in its natural use, by the unnatural use is when I snort it up my nose or shoot it in my arm. I produce only negative results.

Now I'm controlled by an unseen force. I begin to hurt people because this unseen force is telling me to do whatever I need to do to obtain that cocaine.

Then I moved to heroin. Now I'm doing 3 different drugs at the same time. I begin to curse my mother, disrespect women, was almost killed too many times. My lifestyle made the law. Those who are supposed to protect and serve want to kill me. We are talking about a 15 year old kid. But you say that there is nothing wrong with a little indulges.

You better wake up. I lived and eat this stuff. It altered my thinking ability, was slowly destroying my body daily, caused me to hurt people to have it and you have the boldness to say that this is something natural. Is it natural for me to hurt myself or my kids? Is it natural for me to not being able to think straight? Is it natural for me to drop out of school? Is it natural for me to steal or sell my body?

I mean this is the natural response to one who uses drugs. Their bodies drive them to do these things. Is it natural or unnatural?

Negative Reactions

Now that you know some of the things that drugs make you do while on them. Now we will deal with the other negatives reactions that your body will experience when you withdraw from the drug.

When you withdraw from using heroin and barbiturates it can produce chills, fever, convulsions, tremors, vomiting, seizures, diarrhea, sever aches and pains, and cramps.

The withdrawal from stimulants leads to fatigue, irritability, depression, apathy and disorientation.

Narcotics or opiates are drugs which come from opium which are used in the western society. The effects are lethargy, nausea, constipation, drowsiness and slowed respiration. Narcotics carry a high risk for both psychological and physical dependence (Jaffe, Knapp, & Ciraulo, 1997).

Overdose is a great danger with heroin and is the blame for over 4,000 deaths per year in the United States.

Cocaine

Cocaine is an organic substance extracted from the cocoa shrub, which grows mostly in South America. Cocaine produces a very brief high (20-30 minutes unless you take more), while on the other hand a speed high can last many hours (Gold, Miller, & Jonas, 1992). Stimulants produce euphoria very different from that created by Narcotics or sedatives. They produce a buoyant, elated, enthusiastic, energetic, "I can conquer the world!" Side effects are increased blood pressure, sweating, restlessness and muscle tension. Cocaine suppresses appetites and disrupts sleep. This leads to poor eating and sleeping which will result in deterioration in physical health. Moreover, it can cause heart attacks, strokes, and other forms of cardiovascular disease. It leads to paranoia. I can attest to some of these side effects when I was on these drugs.

Marijuana

This drug has subtle effects on emotions, perception and cognition (Grinspoon & Bakalar, 1997).

Emotionally the drug creates a mild and relaxed state of euphoria. This drug carries carcinogens and impurities into the lungs, increasing one's chances for respiratory and pulmonary diseases, and probably lung cancer (Stephens, 1999).

Women who smoke during pregnancy have children with lower birth weight (Zuckerman et al., 1989).

Ecstasy

Problematic side effects include increased blood pressure, blurred vision, insomnia, muscle tension, sweating and transient anxiety (Grilly, 2002). Heavy use of this drug leads to depression, sleeping disorder, elevated anxiety and hostility (Morgan, 2000).

CHAPTER 4 The Problem verses the Solution

    I remember a story that ended in tragedy. A man once came home and walked into his bedroom and caught his girl having sex with another man. He acted off of emotions and killed them both and now is spending the rest of his natural life in prison.

    What was the problem and what the solution? The problem was his girl. The solution was to walk away. Because if she is having sex with another man while you are free. What do you think she will do when you are in prison? That woman has a divided heart. She will cause you trouble. She is not your girl. She is doing what she wants to do so leave her there alive.

    There are more than enough good women for a good man. Think before you react. You have too much at stake. She fell out of love with you. Because if she loved you she wouldn't put you in a harmful situation like that so be smart and never react before you think the whole situation through.

    You must always remember this. Is that intimate relationships aren't designed to stress you out. They are designed to help you propel forward in life.

    This is one of the reasons I am against women flirting. Because when you flirt with a man you make him think something can happen sexually between you two when nothing can. Many rapes take place as a result of this (Lim & Roloff, 1999). You can flirt with a guy so much until he takes the initial act to flirt back with you when your boyfriend is around. You don't want your mate to know what you are doing. So you will resist this guy. May be he'll expose you. Then this could lead to him and your boyfriend getting into a conflict. For what! You're immature ways.

    You have a man at home. Go home and flirt with him, you wonder why you have problems within your relationship. The solution is to stop flirting.

    You may have that kind of man who beats on you for any little thing. I don't agree with this, but you are provoking him. Your actions (the female) could lead to him kicking, biting, punching, choking, slapping or pushing you. This is physical abuse. While he is putting his hands on you, he could be psychological abusing you. This includes name calling or humiliating you.

Psychological abuse also means controlling what your mate does and with whom they socialize with, refusing to communicate with them, or questioning their sanity or unreasonable withholding money.

85% of nonfatal violent crimes committed by intimate partners and in 75% of murders by spouses (Rennison & Welchans, 2000). Partner abuse is a problem (Magdol et al, 1998).

If you want my advice I'll give it to you. Relationships weren't designed to be up and down. The both of you have a role to play. You must learn your role and play it. If you know (which you should) your job is to stimulate your mate's mind, then do it. If she loves looking at your chest, then keep that chest nice and right for the baby. If he loves looking at you from the back, then keep that thing nice and tight. Then just stand in front of him with your hands on your hips and stick that thing up.

My ex and I had this going. I knew it stimulated her mind when I wear a wife beater (a muscle shirt) because of my physique. I knew she liked to stare at me for long periods of time. She knew I liked to look at her from the back. So when I acted crazy. She would stand in front of me with her hands on her hips. My mind would get all the way right. But times came when she didn't want me looking at her. She would act funny and I would act funny but it only pulled is farther apart.

When a woman uses what she knows you like against you. It leads to trouble within that relationship. Regardless of what happened between the two of you. You both still have roles you have to play. The two of you could have had a disagreement about who will cook. Your job is to still stimulate him or her mentally.

The problem is the two of you will have more disagreements. The solution is to be a lady or gentlemen about it and still do the right thing.

I wouldn't advise a man to fall I love with a woman who has had and is having sexually dealings with a lot of different men. Rather she is making them pay or not. She has opened herself to these men and they can disrespect her at any time, especially when you're not around. They know she is a whore and looks at her as that. This is why they only really communicate with her when they want to sexual dealings with her. She gets so accustom to making money until she begin to tease those same men to get more money from them.

This person is dying inside. She wonders why she can't find a good man. Why would I want to marry someone like you? When and if I want to do you anything I want, I only have to give you a few dollars. You know I have a wife at home, but you still give me your dignity for a few dollars. I feel you'll do the same thing to me.

So why would I fall in love with you? If she doesn't change she will cause you so much pain. I'm a living witness.

The problem is her ways. The solution is not to fall in love with her unless she is willing to become the lady I speak about in another chapter. If she doesn't become the lady then soon you could get ready for some serious mental abuse which might lead to your death. This isn't a game. Your life is at stake. You better think with your head and not your penis. You'll save yourself a lot of pain.

In conclusion, if men are dealing with your girl in disrespectful ways, this is because she is allowing it. People respond to you how you allow or train them to. If a woman out of the way approaches me and tries to touch on me. My girl wouldn't have to say or do anything because when I finish with her. I promise I'll never have that problem again. It's supposed to be the same with the women.

CONCLUSION

This book offers spiritual principles to a many dying people. This book is written to develop the man and the woman into what our society needs to once again produce that strong binding family.

Bibliography

1. Wells,1998 Cardiovascular Toxicology, Third Edition, edited by Daniel Acosta Jr, Cited from page 409,Daniel Acosta , Published 2001 by Taylor & Francis.

2. Howard et al., 1998, c Wild, S, Pierpoint, T., Mckeigue, P and Jacobs, H. (2000), cardiovascular disease in women with polycystic ovary syndrome at long- term follow- up: a retrospective cohort study. Clinical Endocrinology, 52: 595-600. Doi: 10.1046/; 1365. 2000.01000. X. article first published online: 24 Dec 2001

3. Lash TL, aschengrau A. 14. A null association between active or passive cigarette smoking and breast cancer risk. Breast Cancer Res Treat. 2002 Sep; 75 (2): 181-4. Us National Library of Medicine national Library of Medicine National Institutes of Health.

4. Lamp et al., Psychology applied to Modern life: adjustment in the 21st Century, Wayne Weiten/ Margaret A. Lloyd. Wadsworth publishing. 2006. Seventh edition.

5. Vanderplate, aral & Magder, 1998, Essentials of abnormal Barlow, Vincent Mark Durand- psychology- 2005 VanderPlate, C. aral. S.O., 81 Magder, L. 1998. The relationship among genital herpes simplex virus, stress, and social support. Health… J.l, stoker, P.B. (1998). Page 645.

6. Marlene's & Sheiham, 1992, cited on page 22. The relationship between work stress and oral health status. By WS Marcenes – 1992- cited by 123- Dec; 35 (12): 1511-20 of social Science & Medicine. Journal – Elsevier

7. Maok & anton, 1999; wood et al. 2001, psychopharma cogenetics- page 195. The role of stress in alcohol use. By Philip Gorwood, Michel D. hamon, Published by Springer

8. Brannon, 1976, Pleck 1995). Psychology applied to Modern Life: adjustment in the 21st century. (Gender- Role Expectations) by Wayne Weiten, Margaret A. Lloyd the 7th Edition, 2006. Wadsworth publishing.

9. Brannon, 1976; Jansz, 2000, 5 Key attributes constitute the traditional male role, the book Psychology applied to modern Life: adjustment in the 21st century, 2006.

10. Joseph Pleck, 1995 Psychology applied to Modern Life: adjustment in the 21st Century, 2006, 7th edition by Wayne W & Margaret A. L.

11. Connell, 1995; I Harris, 1995, Study of African American female college Students .... Nation of hegemonic masculinity. S in which sports plays a defining role.

12. Levant, 1996 the Masculinity Crisis. RR Levant- The journal of Men's Studies Review, Levant, R.E. (1996). The connection between men and women. The Levant. R.E. & Kopecky, G. (1995-96) =. Masculinity reconstructed: chang- Levant R.E & Pollack. W.S. (1995)

13. Christopher Kilmartin, 2000, the Masculine Self Christopher T Kilmartin – 9781597380249. Fourth Edition. Sloan Publishing.

14. Cleek Pearson, 1985 People's Reasons for Divorcing Journal of Family Issues. Cleek. M G., & Pearson, T.A. 1985. Perceived causes of divorce: an analysis of interrelationships.

15. Strasberg etc. al .1994; Van Houten, 1983. Corporal Punishment by Parents and associated child Behaviors. Copy right 2002 by the American Psychological association. Inc. Elizabeth Thompson Gershoff. Psychological Bulletin 2002. Vol. 128 No ., 539-579

16. Weiss et al., 1992 Corporal Punishment in schools and its Effect on academic success. Testimony by Donald E. Greydanus.

17. Berkowitz, 1993 aggression: Its causes, consequences, and control. New York: McGraw-Hill

18. Strasberg, Lowe, 1995 Handbook For Conducting Research on Human Sexuality edited by Micheal W. Wiederman, Bernard E. Whitley. Jr. Page 107

19. Hatfield Rapson, 1996, Love and Sex : Cross-Cultural Perspectives : Needham Heights, MA : allyn & Bacon

20. Daniluk, 1998; Pope, Phillips, olivardia 2000, Measuring male Body Image: A review of the current... Psychology of Men & Masculinity 2004 vol.5 No 1, 18-29. Copyrighted 2004 by the Educational publishing foundation.

21. Christopher Sprecher, 2000, the marriage and family Experience; intimate Relationships in a changing society. By Bryan Strong. Christine Devault, Theodore Cohen. Cengage Learning. Page 204

22. Treas & Giesen, 2000, Sexual infidelity among Married and Cohabiting Americans .by J Treas-2000. Article first published online. 2 mar 2004 Volume 62, Issue 1 pages 48-60 Feb 2000

23. O'Neil & O'Neil 1972, the book open marriage, published by M. Evans & Company. Chapter 16.

24. Thompson, 1984 The Marriage and Family Experience Intimate Relationships in a changing Society. by Bryan strong, Christine Devault, Theodore Cohen, Page 206 Types Of Infidelity

25. David Schnarch, 1997, Passionate Marriage: keeping Love And Intimacy alive Committed Relationships

26. Bell, Weinberg, & Hammersmith, 1981, Sexual Preference alan P. Bell Martin S. Weinberg, Sue Kiefer Hammersmith. Published in 1981. Indiana University Press

27. Patterson, 1992 CJ Patterson. Child development 63c5) 1025-1042

28. Block, 1980, Psychological resilience Wikipedia, the free encyclopedia. Block J.H., & Block J (1980)

29. Argyle & Henderson, 1984, Chapter 7 Friendships across the life cycle.

30. Hochschild, 1997 arlie R. Hochschild/ UC Berkeley Sociology Department. "The Time Bind ; When work becomes home and home becomes work, New York

31. Milkie & Pettola, 1999, Melissa Milkie Publications. Bianchi, S. and Milkie, 2010 Work and Family research. Journal of Marriage And Family

32. Crouter et al., 1999, Mismatch in working hours and affective commitment Research Gate by JH Van Emmerih- 2005

33. Walker, 1994 Men, Women, and Friendship ; Gender & Society, by K Walker Vol.8

34. Fehr, 1996,2000, Friendship Processes- Beverley Anne Fehr; Sage Publications, 1996- Family & Relationships

35. Wright, 1982 Grender differences in same sex friendships- P H Wright 1982.

36. Caldwell & Peplau, 1982 Psychology of Men

37. Davidson & Duberman, 1982, Gender Role orientation and Relational Closeness- Self-Disclosure

38. Levine & Lombardo, 1984 Correlates of cross-sex friendship satisfaction in Hong Kong adolescents. Published by Sage.

39. Rigotti Lee, Wechsler, 2000, Tobacco use by Massachusetts public college students; long term effect of the Massachusetts Tobacco control Program, 2002, June 11. N. Rigotti, S. Regan, N Majchrzak, J. Knight, and H. Wechsler

40. Schlaadt & Shannon, 1994 Drugs: Use, Misuse and abuse by Richard G. Schlaadt and Peter T. Shannon, 1994, Paper back. ISBN- 10: DI32204509

41. Schmitz, Jarvik, & Schneider, 1997, Cognition at Risk : Gestalt Feature Intensive Processing and Cigarette smoking in college students by Justin L. Matthews

42. Baker et al, 2000, Clinical Practice Guideline. Treating Tobacco use and Dependence, 2008... Fiore MC, Jaden CR, Baker TB, et al.

43. Thun, apicella, & Henley, 2000, Global Burden of Disease and Rish Factors, edited by alan D. Lopez, page 247. World Bank Publication.

44. Avanian & Cleary, 1999, Nicotine & Tobacco Research Volume 6, Supplement 3 (Dec .2004) 5333-5340

45. Wells, 1998, Lung Cancer from passive smoking at work. Am J Public Health. 1998

46. Howard et al. 1998 The Normalization of 'Sensible' Recreational Drug use :

47. Lash & aschengrau, 1999, research – based web Design & Usability Guidelines page 473

48. Stoddard & Miller 1995, the Cost of Environmental Tobacco Smoke (ETS): an International Review. J.J Stoddard, T Miller- Review J.J Stoddard, T Miller- American Journal of Epidemiology, 1995

49. Samet, 1992, Health Effects of Exposure to Radon: BE IR , VI Page 462

50. Wechsler et al. 1994, Health and behavioral consequences of binge drinking in college. It National Survey of students at 140 campuses.

51. Wood, Vinson, & Sher, 2001 Handbook of Emotion Regulation, First Edition- edited by James J. Gross

52. Yi et al, 1999, Module 1 ; Epidemiology of alcohol problem in the United States

53. Kinney& Leaton,1987, A Handbook of Alcohol Information by Jean and Gwen Leaton Kinney (Paperback-1987)

54. Wechsler et al, 1994, What we have learned from the Harvard School of Public Health college alcohol study; Herny Wechsler, PH.D, and Toben F. Nelson, SC.D

55. Maisto, galizio & Connors, 1995, Drug use and abuse ; Stephen A. Maisto, Mark Galizio, Gerard J Connors 2nd edition

56. Mathew et al, 1993, psychology applied to Modern Life: adjustment in the 21st Century by Wyane Weiten, Margaret Lloyd, page 459

57. Brownell & Wadden, 2000, Contemporary Clinical Psychology by Thomas G. Plante. Wiley publishing. Page 309

58. Jeffery, 2001, Mokdad et al, 1999, cited on page 93. Obesity, Transportation and land use, is there a connection – Transportation Department North Central Texas Council of Governments

59. Bender et al, 1999, Allison et al, 1999 the impact of obesity on active Life Expectancy in order American Men and Women. SL Reynolds, Y Saito ... 2005- gerontologist.oxfordjournals.org

60. Must et al, 1999, PI-Sunver, 1995, the effects of obesity, smoking, and drinking on Medical problems and costs. R Sturm-Health affairs, 2002 Health affairs.

61. Wing & Polley, 2001, Psychology applied to Modern life: adjustment in the 21st Century by Wayne W. and Margaret A. L, 2006.

62. Rodin et al, 1989 psychology applied to Modern life: adjustment in the 21st century. By Wayne Weiten and Margaret A. LLody. 2006, Hill & Peters, 1998, from the same college book.

63. The following are cited from following Book; Psychology applied to Modern life; adjustment in the 21st Century , by Wayne Weiten and Margaret A LLody , 2006 ;Kant et al., 2000; Stamler et al 2000; Ludwig et al., 1999; Wolk et al; 1999, Messerli Schmieder & Weir, 1997, Lovallo et al, 1990 Rose , 1997, Wynder et al., 1997; Reddy, 1999; Fahey & Gallagherallred, 1990; Lonn & Yusuf, 1997

64. Werbach, 1988 The College book Psychology applied to modern Life; adjustment in the 21st century. Wayne Weiten and Margaret A.L.2006

65. Lumann et al, 1994, the college book psychology applied to Modern Life; adjustment in the 21st Century. Wayne W. Margaret A.L. 2006

66. Hatfield & Rapson, 1996; Thompson, 1983; Buunk, 1980 the college book psychology applied to modern life: adjustment in the 21st century; Wayne W. Margaret A. L. 2006.

67. Lim & Roloff, 1999, Gillen & Muncher, 1995, The College book psychology applied to modern life, adjustment in the 21st century: Wayne W. and Margaret A.L. 2006.

68. Verderber and Verderber, 2001; Mchay et al, 1995 the college book psychology applied to modern life. Adjustments in 21st century: Wayne W. and Margaret A. LLody. 2006, 7th edition.

69. Kleinke. 1986; Matsumoto, 1996; Harrigan et al., 1991 the college book psychology applied to modern life. Adjustment in 21st century Wayne W. and Margaret A. LLody, 2006.

70. Ekman 1975; Cleek & Pearson 1985, the college book psychology applied to modern life, adjustment in 21st century Wayne W. and Margaret A.L, 2006.

71. Stewart. Cooper, Stewart & Friedley, 1988, the college book psychology applied to modern life, adjustment in 21st century Wayne W. and Margaret A. L, 2006.

72. Patterson 1988; the book college psychology applied to modern life, adjustment in 21st century Wayne W. Margaret A. L, 2006.

73. Robert Sternberg's 1986; 1988; the college book psychology applied to modern life, adjustment in 21st century. Wayne W. and Margaret A. L. 2006.

74. Bower & Bower 1991; the college book psychology applied to modern life. Adjustment in 21st century Wayne W. Margaret A. L. 2006.

75. Choice & Lamke 1997, Brown 1993 Barnett & Lamke, 1997, Barnett & Laviolette, 1993 Demaris & Swinford 1996; The College book psychology in 21st century Wayne W.MargaretA. L.2006.

76. Dion& Dion, 1988, Peplau, Hill, & Pep; au 1976, Hill, 1981, Peplau & Gordon 1985, Didia & Allen 1992; cited on page 155. The college book psychology applied to modern life. Adjustment in 21st century. Wayne W. and Margaret A. L, 2006.

77. Eric Berne, 1964 The College book psychology applied to modern life. Adjustment in 21st century. Wayne W. and Margaret A. L. 2006.

78. Cindy Hazen & Phillip Shaver, 1987; the college book psychology applied to modern life. Adjustment in 21st century Wayne W and Margaret A. L, 2006.

79. Wright & Contrada, 1986, Berschid & Walster, 1978, henny, 1994; the college book applied to modern life. Adjustment in 21st century Wayne W and Margaret A. L, 2006.

80. Theodor Reir; The college Book psychology applied to modern 21st century Wayne W and Margaret A. L, 2006.

81. Brehm & Brehm, 1981, Williams et al, 1993, The College book psychology applied to modern 21st century Wayne W and Margaret A. L, 2006.

82. Ialdini, Brehm,1966; The college book psychology applied to modern 21st century Wayne W and Margaret A. L. 2006

83. Jaffe Knapp & Ciraulo, 1997 Stephens 1999, Zuckerman et al, 1989, Grilly, 2002 Morgan 2000, the college book psychology applied to modern life adjustment in 21st century. Wayne W and Margaret A. L. 2006.

84. Lim & Roloff 1999; the college book psychology applied in modern life. Adjustment in 21st century. Wayne W and Margaret A. L. 2006.

85. Rennison & Welchans 2000, Magodol et al, 1998, The College book psychology applied in modern life adjustment in 21st century. Wayne W and Margaret A. L. 2006.

86. Robert Sternberg's, 1986, 1988; the college book psychology applied to modern life. Adjustment in 21st century. Wayne W and Margaret A. L, 2006.

87. All bible verses are taken from the Dake's annotated Reference Bible 2001@ holders Finette Dake Kennedy, annabeth Dake Germaine, and finis Dake, Jr, Dake Publishing
88. Greek and Hebrew translations taken from the Strong's comprehensive concordance of the bible.
89. I looked up every psychologist's in the book and attempted to find out the source of the quotes. This I did to bring honor to them, but I actually retrieved their informational quotes from, all of them from one book. The college book psychology applied to modern life: adjustment in the 21st century. By Wayne Weiten/ Margaret A. LLody, 2006. Published by Wadsworth publishing.

About The Author

Glenn C. Damond, Jr, is an inspirational speaker and a relationship Guru among other thing. He has spoken in different settings to different groups of people. His advice has helped rejuvenate many relationships for over 10 years.

He has completed the school of Christ international, under the leadership of B. H. Clendennen. In addition, he has received 24 hours of college of revivals' Bible College (In addition to over 25 more hours of college credits0, making an A in the ultimate marriage class.

In addition, this book covers work & entertainment principles, which the author has over 18 hour credits in the Entertainment field. This book has business principles. The author recently completed 2 business classes: Business office 7 Intro into B=business. The author earned an A& B in these classes.

Mr. Damond is currently still in college, majoring in Entertainment, and is currently enrolled and active in a Marriage and Family class. The Professor, after hearing of this book, has asked the author to be assertive in the class.

Glenn C. Damond's Next Book

The Other side of Me

(If the man fail to properly dress and keep the woman, she could turn around to destroy him and a nation) (Genesis 2:15; 3:4-6)

A peek inside the next book

The following content will change, in that more chapters, will be added. The author just hasn't named those extra completed chapters

CONTENTS

Section 1: What's becoming of the woman?

1. The origin of Women......
2. The faithful Woman........
3. The Queen........
4. The Queen ....(Part 2)
5. The Queen..... (Part 3)

Section 2: The Dangerous Woman

6. The Strange Woman……
7. The Strange Woman….. (Part 2)
8. Based On True Stories……
9. Based On A true Story (Part 2) The biblical account
10. The Conflict

Section 3: The epitome of Destruction

11. Soul Ties …. (Are you really in love?)
12. Control Issues……
13. Deceptive Emotions…..
14. Another Realm…..
15. Another Realm….. (Part 2)
16. Powerful Agitations……

Section 4: Now that you can see the solution what is your next move?

17. Experience Verses Wisdom
18. How to be set free and stay free

Plus Much More.

ADDITIONAL INFORMATION

Mr. Damond offers counsel sessions for couples or singles, and offers to speak in engagements, churches, church conferences, conferences or seminars. Please contact for booking Mr. Damond at the following:

1. Office: 504-407-5219
2. Virtual assistant: 504-491-2754

Email: glenndamond2@gmail.com.

To place an order of the book, Visit the website at:

http://www.gcdproductions.com

www.ingramcontent.com/pod-product-compliance
Lightning Source LLC
Chambersburg PA
CBHW071707090426
42738CB00009B/1695